Cromwell's
Masterstroke

Cromwell's Masterstroke

The Battle of Dunbar 1650

Peter Reese

Pen & Sword
MILITARY

First published in Great Britain in 2006 by
Pen & Sword Military
an imprint of
Pen & Sword Books Ltd
47 Church Street
Barnsley
South Yorkshire
S70 2AS

ISBN: 1-84415-179-4
ISBN: 978-1-84415-179-0

A CIP catalogue record for this book is
available from the British Library

Typeset in 11/13pt Ehrhardt by Concept, Huddersfield
Printed and bound in England by CPI UK

Pen & Sword Books Ltd incorporates the Imprints of Pen & Sword Aviation, Pen &
Sword Maritime, Pen & Sword Military, Wharncliffe Local History, Pen & Sword
Select, Pen and Sword Military Classics and Leo Cooper.

For a complete list of Pen & Sword titles please contact
Pen & Sword Books Limited
47 Church Street, Barnsley, South Yorkshire, S70 2AS, England
E-mail: enquiries@pen-and-sword.co.uk
Website: www.pen-and-sword.co.uk

Contents

To Jennifer

Maps

Illustrations

Preface

The Battle of Dunbar on 3 September 1650 was the last full-scale engagement between the armies of England and Scotland to take place on Scottish soil. It also marked the turning point in a conflict which, although caused by the previous civil wars, was in fact between two separate countries, the England of Cromwell and the Commonwealth, and Scotland governed by a Covenanting party favouring Charles II as their monarch (provided he acknowledged the Covenant and accepted the dictates of the party). While during the next century there were further clashes, both in Scotland and south of the border, these were between Jacobites and government troops, in which supporters of the displaced House of Stuart attempted to help it regain its royal powers at the expense of the reigning Hanoverians. Even so, if the Jacobite army had continued its march towards London rather than halting at Derby, the political results could have been momentous for both nations.

As a battle, Dunbar ranks with other great clashes between the two nations, such as that at Flodden in 1513 between Henry VIII's general, the Earl of Surrey, and James IV of Scotland, or that at Pinkie Cleugh in 1547 between the Protector, Somerset, and the Earl of Arran. During the three or more centuries of conflict (before the Union of the Crowns in 1603), and in spite of glorious military episodes under Wallace and Bruce, Scottish commanders and their levies generally struggled to preserve their country's sovereign powers against their larger and more powerful neighbour.

So, in 1650, after the execution of Charles I followed by Cromwell's ruthless and successful campaign against Ireland for favouring Charles's son, the chances of Scotland being able to hold out against him and his fearsome Ironsides did not seem high. In reality, having invaded Scotland during the summer of 1650, it was Cromwell and his army who were severely tested, and no other English victory against the Scots was as surprising as that of Cromwell at Dunbar, in a battle where his powers as a commander burned more brightly than ever before and – unlike such relatively haphazard, if heroic, encounters during the early Civil Wars at Edgehill, Marston Moor and Naseby – he was in full command throughout the battle.

For this reason alone the battle deserves further consideration; but, apart from any new examination of its strategic implications, the comparative performances of the opposing commanders and the nature of their differing weapons, Dunbar is also notable because it heralded the development in Britain of what had become widespread in Europe during the previous century, that is, the use of regular standing forces rather than the levies traditionally recruited north of the border. It also merits closer examination because of the growing interest in the final phases of the Civil Wars reflected in a number of recent publications, notably John Grainger's first full-length book on the Anglo-Scottish war of 1650–52, *Cromwell Against the Scots*, published in 1997, together with Raymond Campbell Paterson's book *A Land Afflicted* (1998), which gives an unashamedly pro-Scottish account of the country's Covenanter wars of 1638–90, while in 2004 came Trevor Royle's magisterial overview, *Civil War: The Wars of the Three Kingdoms 1638–1660*. The Battle of Dunbar has a pivotal place within the catalogue of these conflicts, although in these publications it is understandably given relatively short treatment.

The main problem facing any would-be commentators on the Battle of Dunbar is the shortage of contemporary observers. This is often the case with medieval battles and not uncommon even for those of the seventeenth century; it is most marked in the case of Dunbar for, like the earlier Battle of Flodden, which also concluded with a sweeping English victory, there is virtually nothing written from the Scottish viewpoint and the English accounts are hardly numerous. The main sources for Dunbar are Cromwell's own letters (compiled and published by Thomas Carlyle in 1846); a so-called *True Relation of It* by the Puritan soldier Captain John Hodgson (written some twenty years after the event), which includes lists of Scottish prisoners; a short narrative by Cadwell, the first English messenger sent off after the battle; the *Harleian Manuscript*, including a secret service document compiled after interviews with Scottish prisoners following the battle; comments in *Mercurius Politicus*, an early London newspaper; and a lithograph of the battle subsequently produced for Oliver Cromwell by a soldier of fortune, Fitz-Payne Fisher.

From these sources, commentators such as Carlyle agreed upon the main patterns of the conflict (from the English point of view) without considering Fitz-Payne Fisher's lithograph as a serious aid.

Towards the end of the nineteenth century came another burst of interest. In 1897 Professor Samuel Gardiner included a description of the battle in the second volume of his *History of the Commonwealth and Protectorate*, for which he had consulted the Cromwellian expert Charles Firth, who in 1899 gave the most methodical and detailed presentation of it so far to the Royal Historical Society, in which he cited and used Fitz-Payne Fisher's lithograph as a significant authority for the battle's progression. During the previous year the first military history of Cromwell's Scotch campaigns appeared, written by W S Douglas, but, despite its immensely long and dense footnotes, there was little new said about the battle.

In the twentieth century the battle has featured in such books as John Buchan's *Oliver Cromwell* during the 1930s and forty years later in Antonia Fraser's comprehensive work *Cromwell: Our Chief of Men* (1973), although the book which most revealed the nature of the Covenanting armies at Dunbar (building upon an earlier compilation by Charles Sandford Terry) was by Edward Furgol, published in 1990.

With a new century, fresh interest has surfaced in the soldierly aspects of Cromwell's life, as demonstrated in 2004 when the second and third military studies of Cromwell appeared, one by General Frank Kitson (who, however, devoted fewer than five pages to the Battle of Dunbar), and the other by Alan Marshall, an authority on the seventeenth century whose account of the battle is of about the same length.

In the same year came a book by Stuart Reid, published by Osprey, with the battle as its centrepiece. This addressed a number of the battle's more questionable aspects, including the numbers involved and the route taken by Cromwell for his final attack, going so far as to question whether, in the first place, Cromwell intended to destroy the Scottish army rather than attempting himself to escape southward.

Such is the background for the present book, the most comprehensive so far. As with my examination of other battlefields, I start by distinguishing the most influential political and military developments affecting Dunbar and then consider in some detail the patterns of command in both armies and the use of their different weapons systems, before describing the progression of the battle itself. In the process I discover I am at some variance with those who have gone before. For instance, unlike some of the earlier commentators I find it impossible to take Fitz-Payne Fisher's lithograph literally, nor, with Cromwell's need to gain a quick result, together with the actual timescale of the battle, can I see him making a wide sweep before delivering his final assault.

Yet, as with all such battles, whatever the considerations so far, including those in this book, one can be confident the debate about what actually took place on that stormy morning of 3 September 1650 will continue.

Acknowledgements

There are so many people without whose help this book could not have been written. In the first place I am most grateful to Rupert Harding of Pen & Sword Books, who believed I had another battle in me, and to Susan Milligan who so ably edited the final script.

As for others on both sides of the border, in the North I have again enjoyed the remarkable support of the staff both at the National Library of Scotland, including its fine map department, and at the Edinburgh Central Library. With regard to illustrations, I am indebted to the ready assistance of the Scottish National Portrait Gallery.

Where individuals are concerned, at Pitlochry I have received much valuable help from my indefatigable and authoritative friend on medieval artillery, Colonel Tony Guinan, TD; closer to the battlefield, from Pauline Smeed and Roy Pugh, with the Dunbar and District History Society, from Victor Wood at Easter Spott, and from Mrs Sheila Rennie Thomson at Brand's Mill.

In England, the staff of the Army Central Library and the British Library have been most helpful, as well as the staffs of the National Portrait Gallery, the Heinz Archive and Library, and the Ashmolean Museum at Oxford.

As before, most of the writing has taken place within the Prince Consort's Library, Aldershot, where I am 'royally' looked after by chief librarian Tim Ward and all his staff. I have had much assistance from the following: Paul Vickers, military historian and head of the Army Libraries' Information Systems, who has accompanied me on the battlefield and discussed at length the sequence of the conflict before going on to produce excellent battle maps and other illustrations; Dr Leslie Wayper, whose analytical skills and historian's eye remain undimmed; Mrs Jennifer Prophet, who has painstakingly read my first draft and made invaluable observations upon it before, with her son Charles, producing the index; and finally Mrs Christine Batten, whose ability to transfer 'rag tag' longhand into immaculate script – again and again – is wonderful.

Lastly, I would like to thank my wife Barbara who, whenever I was tempted to consider the battle's tactics or even its longer-term effects, to the neglect of the soldiers involved, never failed to show her pity and sympathy for the brave men on both sides who, for whatever reasons, were present on that morning, including those destined to remain there.

Any shortcomings or errors remain, as ever, at my door.

Peter Reese
Aldershot, September 2005

Prologue
1 September 1650

As a cavalryman, David Leslie could think of nothing better than sitting astride a good horse and pursuing a retreating enemy, especially when that enemy was Oliver Cromwell and his fearsome Ironsides. Admittedly, the weather could have been far kinder, but the constant rain and cold winds had so far done more harm to the English than to his own Scottish soldiers. The Covenanting army's commander glanced across at his accompanying staff, hunched in their saddles against the latest squall. Apart from his three eager ADCs awaiting permission to ride ahead, his senior cavalry commander, General Robert Montgomerie, was exchanging comments with Colonel Archibald Strachan, a hard-thrusting rider who was more in sympathy with Cromwell and his sectaries than Leslie would have liked. Not so his senior infantry officer, General James Lumsden, kept fully occupied by a skittish horse, whose usual opinions about the Puritan commander were explosive and unrepeatable.

With Cromwell's army making its best way into Dunbar, watched over by his forward cavalry squadrons, the army commander's party splashed their way through the flooded tracks leading to Doon Hill, that eastern outpost of the Lammermuirs overlooking Dunbar and its adjoining coastal plain. Leslie's main army was not far behind and, once it occupied Doon Hill, would be safe and able to fall upon any English troops attempting to march along the coastal road to Berwick or, alternatively, move down and attack the disease-thinned ranks of the English army close below them.

To prevent Cromwell considering such a southward move, Leslie was about to send one of his cavalry brigades to Cockburnspath, south of Dunbar, where the coastal road passed through a steep defile, thereby effectively blocking off any English withdrawal to Berwick and preventing reinforcements from the south joining them. Leslie had good reason to feel optimistic: from late July he had checked all Cromwell's attempts to occupy Edinburgh and the English had not only been frustrated by his spoiling tactics but had been badly affected by the appalling weather; their numbers were falling from disease and some cracks seemed to be appearing in their morale. The campaign was building to a major battle and, despite his own losses from the Kirk's purges of his army, Leslie seemed to hold much the better hand. He was fully aware of Cromwell's outrageous good luck, as well as his skills in both training and controlling his troops, and in deciding when to take the battlefield initiative – nor, for that matter, could he forget Cromwell's maddening custom of attributing all such decisions to divine guidance.

Whatever inspiration Cromwell might call upon, Leslie was sure any run of luck was bound to come to an end; it had for Charles I's champion, Montrose, following his amazing string of victories during 1645–6, and after Leslie had got much the better of him round Edinburgh the signs were that Cromwell, too, was about to face his reckoning. Besides, Leslie could justifiably feel he also deserved some luck. After distinguishing himself as a young cavalry officer under the leadership of the Swedish warrior king, Gustavus Adolphus (whose own luck ran out in 1632 when he was killed during the Battle of Lutzen), he had been expected to return to Scotland for the coming conflict between the presbyterian Covenanters and their Stuart king, Charles I. Unfortunately, he was severely wounded during the summer of 1640 while serving the Duchess of Hesse and was consequently in no position to join Alexander Leslie's army when it crossed into England nor lead its vanguard (which in other circumstances might well have been his), a privilege that passed to the young James Graham, Duke of Montrose.

When, four years later, the Scots raised another large army in support of the English Parliamentarians and he was appointed commander of the Scottish horse, he found himself placed under Cromwell with his more numerous English cavalry squadrons. At Marston Moor, after Cromwell left the field upon being slightly wounded, Leslie was conscious that he had led the joint cavalry squadrons with great verve, putting the Royalists to flight before sharing in the destruction of the Duke of Newcastle's infantry on Cromwell's return. However, he received virtually no acknowledgement for such great achievements.

In the following year he was detached from the main Scottish army to pursue Montrose, and seizing his opportunity moved rapidly northward until, on 13 September 1645, he caught Montrose when most of his army were away and destroyed his force, although Montrose himself escaped. In April 1650 he completed the task when his leading cavalry detachments under Colonels Strachan and Ker located and defeated Montrose's invaders at Carbisdale in Sutherland, following which Montrose was captured and executed, dying in heroic fashion and as a victim of Charles II's betrayal.

But once again Leslie, who had planned the pursuit and the capture, believed he had received less than his due credit, and it was not until Alexander Leslie, Earl of Leven, reached seventy that he finally got his chance to become the Scottish field commander, and with it the opportunity to make his own decisions (and be more the master of his luck). Leslie knew he had responded well from the time the English crossed the border on 22 July 1650 until he began moving his headquarters towards Doon Hill on 1 September. Very shortly he anticipated having his great battle with Cromwell and, as in other conflicts, such factors as good use of the ground, concentration of one's forces at the key point, surprise and the personal stature of the respective commanders were sure to play their parts. So, too, would that ever unpredictable and elusive element of luck that Leslie could feel he so justly deserved.

Part I

The Disputants

Chapter 1
England and Scotland 1638–1647

> We have no other intention but by our government to honour him and
> for this end to preserve the right and authority wherewith God hath
> vested us.
>
> (Charles I)

The reasons for Cromwell's invasion of Scotland in 1650, and the remarkable Battle of Dunbar in the autumn of that year, lie in the tumultuous twelve years that preceded it. During this chaotic period of general and civil warfare both England and Scotland abrogated the powers of their king, Charles I, and after a series of bewildering twists and turns they finally came to blows, as so often in the past. This appeared all the more remarkable because, in contrast to the late thirteenth and early fourteenth centuries, when England directly challenged Scotland's continuing independence, the seventeenth century promised to end any such military confrontations.

In 1603 the succession of James VI of Scotland to the English throne marked a momentous development in Anglo-Scottish relations. Even though Scotland retained its own parliament, its other political institutions and its customs arrangements, it seemed that Henry VII's hopes for permanent peace between the two countries – for which he had sponsored the marriage between his young daughter Margaret and James IV of Scotland – appeared about to be realized. After more than five centuries of rivalry while England was ruled by Saxon, Norman, Plantagenet, Lancastrian, Yorkist and Tudor monarchs and Scotland first by its Canmore kings then, after Balliol and Bruce, by an unbroken line of Stuarts, the countries shared a common monarch. Furthermore, by the time James VI of Scotland became James I of England they had already been at peace for over forty years, following Scotland's request for help to free it from the clutches of French imperialism.

The advantages of a single monarch soon became apparent when James was able to tackle one of the lasting causes of earlier disputes by transforming the erstwhile lawless border regions of England and Scotland into the middle shires of Great Britain. For families such as the Scottish Humes and the English Percys, it seemed as if their warlike energies would have to be directed elsewhere and if the Humes, for instance, were determined to keep on fighting, like so many others of their kind they would have to look for opportunities beyond Britain. In reality, although the regal union appeared to close off the option of war between the two countries, their distinct and opposing views towards the sovereign, together with strong feelings of national pride reflected in their separate political and legal systems and, above all, their different religious practices, left ample room for friction. In the disputatious mood of the seventeenth century, unless the common sovereign was respected in both countries and his measures equally accepted, any resultant friction could rekindle hostilities between them.

It was religion that provided the spark. Ever since the Reformation religion had frequently meant dissension, but during the early seventeenth century when James became King of England and Scotland it divided the two countries in a way never experienced before. Unlike the High Middle Ages, when the overarching church was recognized by kings and subjects alike and regulated all aspects of society, including trade and industry, there were now several different sects within the Protestant brotherhood vehemently opposed to each other, all of whom felt threatened by the Roman Catholic church in its attempts at counter-reformation. Coinciding with such fissiparous sects came a multiplication of civilian centres of authority, notably through the secularization of extensive estates formerly in the hands of the church. This mood of change and uncertainty was intensified by the ending of monopolies such as trade guilds and by the industrial expansion sparked off by individual merchant adventurers who sponsored new, large undertakings, like Sir George Bruce's vast undersea mine at Culross in Scotland.

In England the Anglican church with its archbishops and bishops offered a measure of continuity by implementing the settlement of Queen Elizabeth and laying down not only what should be believed but how the church should be governed and the nature of its religious celebrations. Its theology was contained in the Thirty-Nine Articles of Religion, including Article Six on Holy Scripture, which confidently proclaimed, 'Holy scripture ordaineth all things necessary to salvation: so, that whatsoever is not read therein, nor may be proved thereby, is not to be required of any man.'[1] In fact, for the determined disputant, varied interpretations about the broad assumptions of Article Six – and the others for that matter – presented a challenge, offering endless opportunity for discussion and dissent. While favouring traditional patterns of worship, the Anglican church left room for different modes of behaviour and, whatever criticisms it faced at the time for its extreme theology, its very moderation in an age of both intolerance and religious zeal gave rise to different and opposed sects operating within its broad parish.

Traditional believers were known as Arminians (after the Dutch theologian Jacobus Arminius), who maintained that God working through the Anglican church could grant forgiveness for all, providing they repented of their sins. Close behind them were the Laudians (after Charles I's Archbishop William Laud), who believed in all the set patterns of thought and worship laid down by the Anglican church and celebrated in its rituals. Both Arminians and Laudians rejected the doctrine of and the prospect of fighting and suffering a defeat over the custody of Charles I was unthinkable. After long negotiations it was eventually agreed the king should be transferred into the hands of the English Parliament, and the Scots were then to be paid £400,000 to compensate them for their heavy expenses since January 1644. (This was to be made in two instalments, but the second was, in fact, never paid.)

In any case, the Scottish army no longer had a role, for only isolated pockets of Royalist resistance remained. After releasing the king on 28 January 1647, Leven ordered his army back to Scotland. The final chapter of a military adventure that had started so well saw it march out of Newcastle to verbal abuse and accompanied by showers of stones from the women of the town. On arriving in Scotland it was reduced to a small core of 5,000 foot and 1,200 horse on the lines of – but as a much smaller version – the English New Model Army. This was considered quite large enough to deal with the remaining centres of Royalist support in Scotland, including Alasdair MacColla MacDonald and his Irish soldiers in the far north-west.

As in the past, by the end of the first Civil War Scotland, the smaller country whose disillusion with its king had brought the descent into hostilities, had come off worse than its neighbour and any resumption of fighting would probably repeat this pattern. Although it had supported the English Parliamentarians against their king in the hope that presbyterianism would spread, this had ended with the rise of Cromwell and the Puritan Independents. Henceforth, any new attempt by Royalists in Scotland to return to their traditional policy of supporting the monarchy risked punitive military actions from a republican Protector and his Puritan soldiers.

The following chapter examines the nature of Scotland's major challenges to the Commonwealth, bringing military responses from Cromwell that were to pave the way for his final invasion of the country, and the pivotal clash between their main armies at Dunbar.

Chapter 2

Auld Enemies Again 1648–1650

It is expected Cromwell shall be clear master of all Ireland as he is of England, and then have at the third poor broken kingdome more easy than any other to be swallowed down.

(Robert Baillie, *Letters and Journals*)

Less than twelve months after handing over the king and disbanding their forces the Scots renewed their support for the monarchy, a decision that led to their need for another large army. Although Charles I was kept under various forms of restricted custody in England this did not prevent him from making continuous efforts to retrieve his position, including opening negotiations with Englishmen still loyal to the Royalist cause and, of course, with the Scots. To help counter such initiatives the English Parliament had drawn up the 'Four Articles', designed to reduce his regal powers greatly; these proposed keeping the militia out of royal control for the next thirty years, abolishing episcopacy, allocating funds in support of the New Model Army and allowing Parliament itself to decide when it would meet.

No seventeenth-century king worth the name would have signed such bills, and the day they were placed before him Charles entered into a new agreement with Scotland (the Engagement) by which he agreed to enforce state presbyterianism in England for an initial three-year period and agreed to work for a closer union between England and Scotland. In return, the Scots undertook to send troops into England to help remove the New Model Army. Despite the widespread dissension in the country at the time, this represented a mammoth and highly dangerous undertaking. During the so-called Second Civil War, the Scottish forces were expected to work in tandem with uprisings from Royalist supporters and with radical elements within the Parliamentarian army, who had become seriously discontented by, among other things, the large amounts of pay still owed to them and by current threats to disband their regiments. Although each regiment had appointed its own representatives, the agitators, they were nevertheless anti-presbyterian.

With the extent of disaffection within the army and the considerable number of Royalist sympathizers (particularly in Wales), if only the Scottish troops had been able to move quickly into England while Cromwell was meeting uprisings in Wales and Parliament's other senior commander, Fairfax, was similarly engaged in East Anglia, the situation might have become very serious for the two leaders. That this never happened was largely due to the slowness of the Scottish mobilization together with Cromwell's and Fairfax's prompt reactions. The Scots began to muster their army on 27 April 1648 but soon ran into serious difficulties when the ageing Leven declined the overall command and David Leslie refused command of the horse. Both were out of sympathy with the Engagers for making an agreement with the king when he offered no more than temporary support for presbyterianism.

Command of the Scottish forces, therefore, went to the Duke of Hamilton who was almost entirely lacking in military experience, while an unimpressive martinet, the Earl of Callendar, was made second in command, with John Middleton the general of horse. Callendar did not co-operate easily, being opposed, for instance, to Sir George Monro, who commanded the formidable Ulster contingents attached to the army, and he was often at odds with Hamilton himself. Added to any deficiencies in its leadership, the army lacked experienced soldiers, with the exception of those 'New-Modelled' the year before and the 2,000 foot and 1,200 horse sent from Ulster. In the circumstances, its target strength of 30,000 was also remarkably optimistic, although from late January both the Committee of Estates and a majority of the Scottish Parliament had favoured some form of alliance with Charles.[1] Not so the Covenanting ministers, whose preaching against 'the Engagement' made recruitment very difficult, especially in Ayrshire. Would-be recruits were regarded by the ministers as morally unsound, while others, appalled by the prospect of a hazardous invasion into England, fled to the hills or even to Ulster. As Bishop Burnet recorded, 'The regiments were not full, many of them scarce exceeded half their number, and not a fifth man could handle a pike. They had no artillery – not so much as a field piece – very little ammunition and very few horses to carry it.'[2]

This far from impressive force had time running strongly against it. When the Duke of Hamilton led it across the border on 8 July 1648 the uprisings in England were already petering out. He had just 10,500 men, not much more than a third of the projected total, although at Carlisle he was reinforced with a further 3,000. Hamilton then compounded his problems by progressing far too slowly, and by the end of the month the uprisings in England and Wales had been crushed, except for those in the south-east. He did not reach Kendal on his intended path to South Wales until 2 August, where Sir George Monro and his Ulster troops joined him. Hamilton now had about 18,000 troops against John Lambert's 9,000 New Model soldiers sent to meet him, but by 13 August Cromwell succeeded in joining Lambert with another 5,000 men, having covered 287 miles in thirteen days. In contrast, Hamilton had taken a month to complete 100 miles. The two sides met at Preston where Hamilton's army, in its attempts to link up with Royalists in Lancashire, was strung out along the road. A running battle followed, the final engagement of which took place at Winwick, near

Warrington, and although the Scottish soldiers fought with their customary tenacity, their leaders were no match for Cromwell and Lambert; by 19 August the uneven fight was over, with 3,000 Scottish soldiers killed and 10,000 taken prisoner against the relatively light casualties sustained by Cromwell's soldiers.

The news of Hamilton's defeat brought serious internal disruptions in Scotland, where there was widespread scepticism about Charles I's true attitude to presbyterianism. After a troop of Scottish cavalry was attacked in Ayrshire by followers of the Earl of Eglinton, anti-Engager Covenanters rose in revolt across the whole south-west of Scotland. Leven and Leslie (both allies of Hamilton's enemy, the Duke of Argyll) took command and under their leadership such zealots marched on Edinburgh in a putsch that became known as the 'Whiggamore raid',[3] only for it to suffer a serious reverse at the hands of Sir George Monro's Ulstermen near Stirling. Although the Engager forces were still stronger than the 'Whiggamores', Cromwell had promised Argyll his military support and having reached the border he was demanding the return of Carlisle and Berwick. At this the Scottish Committee of Estates accepted the inevitable and ordered the governors of Berwick and Carlisle to surrender to him and for Monro to return to Ulster. It did not, however, suit Cromwell at this time to become entangled in any further fighting in Scotland and, ignoring his recent campaign, he sent conciliatory messages to Loudon, chancellor of the new ministry, in which he referred to the concordat struck between England and Scotland during the First Civil War, 'the late dispensation, in gaining so happy success against your and our enemies in our victories, may be the foundation of the union of the people of God in love and unity.'[4]

Cromwell moved his army close to Edinburgh, where he kept it under strict control to avoid offending the local people, and on 4 October Argyll invited him into the city for talks, when he dined with both Argyll and Wariston. Although Cromwell was utterly opposed to the Covenanters' demands for the adoption of presbyterianism in England, it suited him to make peace with the Kirk party because of his more pressing concerns with the king. During their conversations Cromwell and Argyll agreed to all Engagers being removed from positions of power and for the Scottish army to be disbanded once more, except for a small force of 1,500 men under Leven's direction. Sir James Turner has suggested that in addition they discussed 'a necessity to take away the King's life', but whether this was so or not, after three days Cromwell returned south leaving Lambert and two English regiments to help Argyll's Kirk party establish itself fully.

Back in England Cromwell began a leisurely siege of Pontefract Castle and he did not, in fact, return to London until 6 December, on which day the New Model Army's Colonel Pride prevented from entering the House of Commons 140 members of the English Parliament in favour of an accord with the king. By the end of the month Cromwell had decided the king should be tried (and condemned) – 'I tell you we will cut off his head with the crown on it'[5] – and the remainder of the Commons (the Rump) duly agreed to a court being set up to try Charles Stuart, 'the man of blood'.

Whatever faction held power in Scotland, the country would always be more monarchical than Cromwell and his sectarian supporters, and during January 1649 the limitations of the latest agreement between them became apparent when the Scottish Committee of Estates wrote to the English Parliament stressing that no action should be made against the king without the agreement of the Scottish Parliament. Scottish commissioners travelled to London where on three occasions they condemned the arraignment of the king until, on 29 January, they sent a final appeal on the sovereign's behalf to Fairfax. 'We entreat that you will take into serious consideration that the Kingdome of Scotland hath undoubted interest in his Majesty's person, and how hard a thing it is to proceed against their King, not only without but against their advice and consent.'[6] On 30 January 1649 the king was beheaded. With his death the temporary understanding arrived at between Cromwell and Argyll ended, and the way was opened for further hostilities between England and Scotland.

On 5 February 1649, six days after Charles I's execution, the Scottish chancellor, John Loudon, standing at Edinburgh's mercat cross proclaimed the Prince of Wales King of Great Britain and for good measure acknowledged his regal authority over France and Ireland as well. Such provocative action was an expression of Scotland's fury at England's unilateral decision to execute the man who was also their king, although the Scots took the precaution of suspending confirmation of Charles II's title to the crown until he signed the National Covenant. Notwithstanding, Loudon's proclamation presented a direct challenge to Cromwell's England which, since 4 January, had called itself a Commonwealth, thus giving Cromwell cause to wage his final two campaigns – in Ireland and Scotland – aimed at crushing all remaining opposition within the home countries.

In the meantime Ireland had also made overtures to Charles II. The Duke of Ormond, in command of an army of 15,000 men and 500 horse, invited him there to help rally further support for the Royalist cause. Faced with opposition on two fronts the English Puritans concluded that Ireland was their most pressing danger, since it constituted a better springboard from which Charles could invade England, and to forestall this they decided to mount an invasion of Ireland themselves. Since January they had been engaged in raising and equipping a suitable army for the purpose, although Cromwell, its unchallenged leader, did not set out for Ireland until 11 July, with his invasion force following on 13 August 1649. Cromwell was commander in chief, with Fairfax holding the more senior, if less active, post as his lord general. Because the English Council of State had decided to attack Scotland as well, the Scottish leaders were bound to be greatly concerned by Cromwell's attack on Ireland.

In the event, they watched Cromwell wage a ferocious campaign aimed both at ending any chance of the Irish invading England and at striking a blow against Catholicism – a campaign that continues to arouse differing reactions today. A recent attempt to justify Cromwell's actions there by drawing attention to his need for an aggressive campaign to finish things with the minimum of expense has been made, for instance, by the Irish writer Tom Reilly.[7] Such reasoning is not completely convincing, because although Cromwell's initial savagery undoubtedly caused the towns of Trim and Dundalk to be abandoned quickly, it also led to subsequent delays: at Waterford the defenders felt they had nothing to lose by fighting on and at Clonmel, in particular, the desperate garrison held out longer than anyone could have reasonably expected. Whatever pressures Cromwell might have been under, the Scots could have been in no doubt about the menace posed to their country by him and his fearsome sectaries.

Besides, whatever the new republic's financial difficulties, Cromwell had taken pains to see his army had ample funds not only to establish a good intelligence service (by paying informers well) but to supply ports along the English west coast with large quantities of food for rapid shipment to Ireland.[8] In truth Cromwell's expedition to Ireland was more than a military operation; it was a crusade in which he fully believed that 'with such a cause extreme severity was a right and duty.'[9] Following his victories, he removed the native Irish to the barren lands of Connaught or overseas so that the land could 'be replanted with many noble families of this nation, and of the Protestant religion.' Ireland itself could then 'be put in the hands of good English Protestant stock and a purged Ireland would emerge from its barbarous priest-ridden chaos.'[10]

It was with such underlying beliefs that he moved against Drogheda, his first military objective, and began by pounding it with heavy guns. After breaches were made in its walls he signalled a general advance, having ordered 'no quarter' since his summons to surrender had been refused. Of the garrison, 2,800 were killed, some of whom had actually surrendered, followed by a further 700 civilians and clergy, all of whom he ordered to be killed. A flagrant example of inhumane treatment of prisoners came three days after the battle, when the Royalist commander, Sir Edmund Verney, while talking with Cromwell, was taken aside by someone he thought of as an old friend only to be run through with a sword and killed. At Drogheda Cromwell's Ironsides lost just 150 men. Any chance of Cromwell using his own small losses as a moral justification for his savagery was seriously compromised since he knew full well that most of the garrison consisted of 'respectable Irish Protestants or Catholics who had opposed the insurgents.'[11] Cromwell was reduced to justifying his behaviour to Parliament by suggesting that Drogheda would deter further resistance and thereby 'prevent the effusion of blood for the future' – which of course did not prove to be the case.[12]

Cromwell's next target of Wexford saw similar slaughter. While its representatives attempted to negotiate a ceasefire Cromwell's soldiers went on killing the defenders, together with any priests they could find. Although he had given no direct orders to this effect, Cromwell made no effort to stop them, nor did he blame his troops afterwards for the deaths of 2,000 people who, in his judgement, fully deserved God's vengeance.

In military terms, the fighting following Drogheda and Wexford was not nearly so bloody, and in his nine-month campaign Cromwell succeeded in gaining control of almost all the country, although a further two years would be needed before all pockets of resistance were destroyed. Cromwell's only major military reverse came at the siege of Clonmel, where his own casualties amounted to 2,000 soldiers, before he eventually gained control there as well.

Whatever conclusions the Scots reached about Cromwell's methods as an invader, they were undoubtedly aware of the high physical toll that the country's climate took on his soldiers. Apart from the army's battle casualties (including the 2,000 suffered at Clonmel), which totalled a third of its original strength of 12,000, there were significant other losses from sickness. The ailments were usually of a temporary nature but some were serious enough to cause death or at least bring their subjects' service to an end. These maladies included dysentery, the scourge of all armies at this time, field malaria and spotted fever (plague). Cromwell himself fell ill at one time and wrote, 'I scarce have one officer of forty amongst us hath not been sick, and how many considerable ones we have lost is no little thought of heart to us.'[13]

Ireland's inhospitable climate and Cromwell's hard driving made such casualties inevitable. On the other hand, the army's successes under him encouraged ample numbers of English veterans to come forward for further campaigns, since the New Model Army had no rival in the British Isles nor, indeed, in the rest of Europe at the time.

With hostilities in Ireland running down, during early 1650 the English Parliament began considering the inevitable war with Scotland and how they could make a pre-emptive strike before the Scots were able to mount their own invasion. Cromwell, however, was in no hurry to rush back to London, even though the demands in Ireland became less urgent, and arrangements were in train for the forces needed for the Scottish campaign. It was not until 1 June that he was welcomed officially on Hounslow Heath, and two days later by the City of London, before, on 4 June, he made his formal report to the House of Commons. Eight days later Parliament appointed the popular Sir Thomas Fairfax as their commander in chief for the Scottish expedition, with Cromwell as his lieutenant general.

After his achievements in Ireland it is highly doubtful whether this decision pleased Cromwell, but on 24 June, the very day on which Charles II (after signing the Covenant) disembarked from the Dutch ship *Skidam* in the Moray Firth, making an invasion of Scotland all the more urgent, a committee of the English Council of State (with the authority to raise an army for Scotland and decide on its leadership) met in the Palace of Whitehall. It had been called together by Cromwell and consisted of four men apart from himself: John Lambert, Thomas Harrison, Oliver St John (married to Cromwell's cousin) and Bulstrode Whitelocke. The main subject for their consideration was whether they could persuade Fairfax, a strong presbyterian, to accept the command of the force directed against presbyterian Scotland, an offer he had already refused because, 'as England and Scotland were joined in a solemn League and Covenant for us to enter into their country with an army and make war upon them is what I cannot see the justice of.'[14] The others, including Cromwell, tried to make him change his mind, Cromwell arguing that the Scots (when under the Engagement) had already invaded England and were busy raising forces and money to repeat the process, concluding 'that there will be war between us, I fear, is unavoidable.' Fairfax again refused, and to help resolve the problem wrote on the next day to the Speaker of the House of Commons, pleading 'debilities both in body and mind'. Cromwell was thereupon appointed both captain general and commander in chief for all the forces raised or to be raised within the Commonwealth of England.

Whether he was sincere or not in his attempts at persuading Fairfax to take the command, with Cromwell in charge there would certainly be no reluctance to wage a vigorous war against the last of his national challengers and Cromwell was undoubtedly the better commander in the circumstances. As historian John Grainger has justly observed, 'It took much more than mere military competence to conduct the Scottish campaign – it needed the ability to argue, to persuade, to intrigue – to be a politician as well as a commander.'[15] In any case, it was Cromwell who had led the movement to execute Charles I and, following his successful campaign in Ireland, he had become the most powerful man in England and could be sure of parliamentary support for a similar campaign in Scotland.

* * * *

Cromwell's problems were minor compared with those facing the men responsible for Scotland's defence. Following Cromwell and Lambert's defeat of the Engagers' army during 1648 and the succession of the Covenanting Kirk party, the Covenanters had to meet a number of serious challenges to their authority before they could concentrate on assembling and training the forces needed to meet Cromwell.

During February a Royalist uprising in the north-east of Scotland had to be put down by David Leslie, and its leader, the Marquis of Huntly, was beheaded in Edinburgh on 22 March. In the same month much the most serious challenge to the Covenanters arose when, from his residence at The Hague, Charles II appointed Montrose as lieutenant governor of Scotland and captain general of his forces there. As a result Montrose sent an advance party to Orkney to recruit men for an invasion in the far north of Scotland and on 9 April his force, consisting largely of inexperienced Orcadians, crossed over to Caithness, where they were surprised and defeated by Leslie's cavalry commander, Colonel Archibald Strachan, at Carbisdale. The Royalists were hunted down, but Montrose, although wounded, escaped, only to be captured a week later. All finally ended for him when, with no intervention by the king on his behalf, he was swiftly tried, condemned to death and beheaded on 21 May, and his body was divided into four quarters. A later uprising, this time by the Gordons, at Dufftown on 8 May 1650, was met and also defeated by Leslie's cavalry.

It was not until May that Charles II signed an agreement recognizing the Kirk party as Scotland's official civil administration and repudiated his support for Ireland, thus ending any hope of religious toleration there.[16] A month later he signed the Scottish Covenant, although when he returned to Scotland, Argyll's continuing doubts about his loyalty to the Covenanters were such that restrictions were imposed both on the king's movements and on any decrees made in his name. Although Charles II had done nothing to save Montrose or any of those with him who invaded Scotland on the king's behalf, the extreme Covenanters were right to distrust their new sovereign, who habitually looked for support among the traditionally Royalist regions of Scotland.

Further evidence of the unsettled state of the country as it prepared for the expected English attack came on 21 June, two days before the king signed the Covenant. Men who were not pious Covenanters, especially those who had previously taken part in past Royalist uprisings or served with the Engagers, were weeded from the army, thus depriving the Scottish military of experienced officers and men at a time when they were sorely needed.

Unlike Cromwell, who had a well-disciplined and unified force for his campaign in Scotland, the Scottish commander, David Leslie, not only faced problems affecting those troops whom the Kirk considered morally unsuitable to man his battle lines, but experienced in his relatively poor country far greater restrictions in financial support and an agonizingly slow system of recruitment, not to mention continuing political interference in his choice of subordinate commanders. In such circumstances it seemed likely that, in spite of the country's strong fighting traditions and the out-standing performances of its commanders at Marston Moor and in Europe during the Thirty Years War, Scotland's current political and religious divisions might well bring military reverses at the hands of the all-conquering Cromwell and his zealous Ironsides.

Whatever the final outcome, the Scots were about to experience again the full effects of an invading army within their own country. Even so, none could have forecast the manner of their encounter with the English at Dunbar on 3 September 1650.

Chapter 3

The English Army and its Commanders

We that serve you beg of you not to own us, – but God alone – for our
successes.   (Oliver Cromwell, *Letters*)

The salient feature of the army raised by the English Parliament during 1650 for its campaign in Scotland was its complement of regular volunteer soldiers. Five of its seven cavalry regiments had, for instance, originally been trained by Cromwell and had then formed part of the New Model Army. In the case of the other two regiments, John Lambert's had been recruited during the early stages of the Civil War as part of Fairfax's Northern Association,[1] while that commanded by Colonel Francis Hacker had been mustered in 1648 and probably recruited largely from among troops with earlier war experience.

Six of these cavalry regiments were formed into two brigades, commanded by Major General John Lambert and Colonel Robert Lilburne, while the seventh came under the direct command of Cromwell himself. The standard English regiments numbered 600 men, with Cromwell's being at least as large, and in addition two companies of dragoons (which had been upgraded to horse) were commanded by Colonel John Okey. The cavalry's establishment totalled 5,400 men, or virtually a third of the total army, and at a muster taken immediately prior to crossing the Scottish border on 22 July 1650 the actual strength of the horse was found to be marginally above full establishment at 5,415;[2] the prospect of again serving with Cromwell had clearly attracted more than enough volunteers.

Of the nine infantry regiments three were directly descended from the New Model Army; the one which Lambert would take over from Colonel John Bright at the start of the campaign had previously served in the old Northern Association; another, which Cromwell created for Colonel George Monck, also came from units that could be traced back to the New Model Army. The same pattern applied to the other four regiments, three of which were raised in 1648, although the fourth was formed later still (originally for service in Ireland). If the latter's connection with the New Model Army was more tenuous, it nevertheless was bound to have a proportion of veterans serving with it.

vinegar or the lees of wine[8]) was brought down into the musket's pan to fire the priming charge, which in turn set off the main one. But the matchlock also had certain serious disadvantages, since it was an uncertain weapon in bad weather, when the match became damp, and one commentator at this time, Sir Thomas Kellie, wrote of seeing the muskets of four men out of ten fail to go off.[9] It also required many movements before firing and the lighted matches carried by the musketeers gave their positions away, especially at night, and large quantities of match were consumed while they waited to fire. However, the alternative firelock musket, which after cocking was ready to shoot, was more complicated to manufacture and therefore more expensive, so that at this time its issue was still limited to soldiers guarding the artillery train or where open supplies of powder were known to be standing.

Although the musketeers were spared the burden of carrying long pikes, their weapons needed a range of cumbersome ancillary equipment, such as a broad leather belt from which a number of containers holding different quantities of pre-measured powder were suspended. Traditionally these containers were twelve in number, popularly likened to the twelve apostles. Musketeers also carried a bag of bullets and a flask, or horn, containing coarse powder. (By this time the cumbersome shaft of wood with a forked top used to support the musket's barrel had been dispensed with.)

Any consideration of the probable tactics open to the English in 1650 must keep the greater efficiency of the infantry in mind. The increased proportion of musketeers (two to each pikeman) and the growing effectiveness of their weapons gave the infantry a greater hope of withstanding a cavalry charge when musketeers and pikemen combined, but this was something that required good discipline and prolonged training. Earlier the New Model Army, following the examples of Gustavus Adophus and Montrose, had reduced its depth of ranks from ten to six and begun to consider reducing them further to three, where all three were capable of firing at the same time, and this practice was probably followed by Cromwell's infantry in 1650.

Other tactics were also being adopted to assist the infantry in the attack; when reaching close quarters with the enemy the musketeers would usually give one or two volleys and then the pikemen would level their weapons and charge home, by which time the musketeers would have taken up new positions on the flanks to fall upon the enemy with their muskets' butts. Infantry tactics in general were becoming more and more aggressive, although it was not until after the Dunbar campaign and the restoration of Charles II that the plug bayonet was adopted,[10] which gave musketeers a real ability to withstand cavalry attacks.

Cavalry tactics were also evolving; for example, in the New Model Army the heavy cuirasses and lances were dispensed with in favour of swords and pistols. From their normal positions on the extreme flanks Cromwell would have them in close order advancing at the trot and reserving their fire until coming to close quarters, following which they were expected to regroup and attack again.

Both cavalry and infantry were supported by artillery, with its complement of 690 all ranks and its considerable train of guns and accompanying carts carrying powder and ammunition. In 1650 there were two roles for such guns: for siege work or deployment in the field. The cannon used for sieges were massive, with projectiles ranging from 30 to 60 pounds, and each gun needed up to thirty-two horses or oxen to draw it, making movement across wet ground an immense task. The Scots reported at the time that Cromwell called his heavy guns 'The Twelve Apostles' and he put 'his whole trust in them'.[11] Those used in the field were smaller, ranging from culverins, with shot of 16 to 20 pounds, demi-culverins with 9 to 12-pound balls, and sakers whose shot weighed 5 to 6 pounds, but each demi-culverin still needed six horses or eight oxen. (Horses were generally more biddable than oxen and able to exert more effort.) Sakers were the guns used most commonly, although there were even lighter types, such as minions and drakes, firing shot of 3 to $3^1/_2$ pounds. By this time some of the sakers had been fitted with trail wheels for easier handling, but only over short distances, and the wheels were removed when the guns were brought into action.[12] The powder for the charges was sometimes made up into cartridges, although it was often kept in barrels standing behind the guns.

Cromwell took pains to see his army was well supported by both siege and field artillery with sufficient men to operate them effectively, and it was likely he allocated two of the lighter field pieces to each of his infantry regiments although, at Dunbar, he took the decision to mass his field artillery.

Guns were usually crewed by three skilled men;[13] along with the gunner himself came his mattross (or assistant gunner) with the third crew member used for fetching and carrying. If Cromwell's cannon (both field and siege) numbered around twenty-two pieces (requiring sixty-six gunners to fire them), this left over 600 other members in the train. A good proportion of these were probably skilled 'artificers' who were required to carry out 'the multitude of tasks needed to keep the guns supplied and moving – including blacksmiths, coopers, wheelwrights, farriers, carpenters and clerks'.[14] The train also had companies of pioneers to clear the roads and construct the necessary bridges. The pioneers would normally have a form of crane, known as a 'gin', to help remount the guns after they had been carried on four-wheeled carriages along the line of march. The artificers' equipment required dozens of carts and wagons and these came under the control of a Wagon Master General; transporting the artillery was a most arduous and complex task, with even as few as two guns requiring a complete 'bye train'.

By now the specialization of the artillery was such that it led the infantry to accuse artillerymen of adopting superior graces. Such men certainly had to follow a strict set of movements while loading their fearsome weapons and there were, for instance, thirteen separate commands for the use of the sponge and the ladle. A gunner also had to be deft and practised, and to 'set forth himself with as comely a posture and grace as he can; for by agility and comely carriage in handling the ladle and sponge doth he give great content to standers by.'[15] However, with Cromwell as commander in chief, there seemed little possibility of his gunners being allowed to adopt too high-flown an attitude at the expense of other arms.

In the earlier stages of the Dunbar campaign artillery was used by both sides during the fighting around Edinburgh, and during such actions while it is just possible that siege pieces were also used, the primitive roads at that time would have made the rapid movement of heavy guns very difficult.

Cromwell's army was also supplied with tents. Despite their use in Ireland during the previous year they were not available at the commencement of his Scottish invasion, although this was remedied quite quickly. Writing to Speaker Lenthall from Dublin on 17 September 1649 Cromwell had emphasized the importance of tentage, telling him, 'We keep the field much; our tents sheltering us from the wet and the cold',[16] but even then he suffered many casualties from dysentery. Scotland was no less wet and generally colder than Ireland – certainly during the autumn of 1650. A month into the Scottish campaign, tents arrived on the scale of one for every six men, carried in parts by the soldiers, and they were the more important because Cromwell savagely punished any soldier who, in whatever attempts he made to get warmth and shelter, damaged civilian property. As in Ireland, the problems caused by the cold and exceedingly wet Scottish autumn took a heavy toll on his men.

The English Commanders
Apart from Cromwell himself, the three most prominent leaders with the English army at Dunbar were Lieutenant General Charles Fleetwood, Major General John Lambert and Colonel George Monck. It was characteristic of Cromwell that among his other officers who commanded brigades, Colonels Robert Lilburne, Thomas Pride and Robert Overton, and Colonel John Okey, a one-time chandler who commanded the dragoons, were men not only familiar with his methods of fighting but who had shared in the singular responsibility of signing Charles I's death warrant.

Oliver Cromwell, Commander in Chief
Oliver Cromwell was not only the greatest figure in seventeenth-century Britain but one of the most remarkable and enigmatic figures in British history: family man, regicide and unbending Calvinist, once he made up his mind he would justify his every action through the words of the Bible. At the time of the Civil War, Cromwell became convinced that England should be governed not by a sovereign employing his divine right to rule, but by senior representatives of the people who were right believers – the good and the wise – in both a political and religious sense, men whom he thought of as 'the people of God'.[17] Among them, of course, stood himself, God's own instrument, who would govern constitutionally – although whether he truly believed in the sovereignty of the people is more questionable, for, as Antonia Fraser has observed, 'as the shadows of the Protectorate lengthened, he found himself using those very expedients, financial or political, against which he had originally protested with Charles I.'[18]

Although both soldier and statesman,[19] of chief interest are his powers as a military leader. As late as 1642, at the age of forty-three, the untidy country gentleman had no knowledge of war. This he was to acquire by reading about other commanders, by watching the conduct of professional soldiers, particularly Thomas Fairfax and Lawrence Crawford with whom he so often disagreed, and, most important of all, by taking part in a number of widely different actions. Conversely, unlike other senior officers, he lacked the prejudices associated with past military conventions and from the outset was able to select like-minded men for his captain's troop and, after ensuring they were properly armed and mounted, train them to his own demanding standards, the full details of which were recorded in the *Samuel Squire Papers*.[20] From becoming a captain of a company he quickly went on to raise a regiment, then to command all the cavalry of the Eastern Association (from East Anglia), before helping to create the New Model Army, a force, in the words of Edward Hyde, Earl of Clarendon, 'whose order and discipline, whose sobriety and manners, whose courage and success made it famous and terrible over the world.'[21] Like Sir John Moore's Light Division 150 years later, Cromwell's vision of creating such a force from the disorderly units at the time and infusing it with his own spirit was to play a vital part in his reputation as a commander.

By 1645 Cromwell had evolved his battlefield techniques, particularly with regard to the cavalry, although he was not to exercise independent command until 1648. During the campaigns of 1648 to early 1650, when he put down mutinies within the New Model Army before defeating the Scottish Engagers' army under James, Duke of Hamilton, and then went on to conquer Ireland, his trademark skills were evident. The energy and aggression evoked by his choleric nature, the rapidity of his movements and concentration of force against an enemy's weakest point are evident, while in Ireland his impatience and ruthlessness, together with his strong reluctance to waste his own soldiers' lives were much to the fore. There, too, he showed his understanding of sea power as a means of supplying his army and moving its heavy ordnance along the coast.

As a commander Cromwell followed Thomas Fairfax's custom of holding councils of war with his senior commanders before major actions, although these did not stop him from energetically pressing his own tactical options. At Dunbar those attending the vital council before the battle, such as John Lambert and George Monck, were by no means 'yes men', but by then they could not doubt Cromwell's moral and physical courage, together with his *coup d'oeil* – the ability to recognize the main chances offered on the battlefield. They also appreciated his willingness to allow them a certain amount of independence, even if keeping a careful watching brief. Fully aware of Montrose's failings in this respect, Cromwell believed strongly in reconnoitring before a battle and often took part in such missions himself. In his desire to learn about what went on over 'the other side of the hill' he was also willing to pay for facts about his opponent's intentions, and later, during the Protectorate, he established an intelligence branch under John Thurloe, which intercepted private correspondence and received letters from agents posted throughout Europe.[22] Conversely, he could be both secretive and devious over his own plans.

Cromwell's campaigns would, in many senses, always be 'holy', in that he sought a just peace and what he believed to be a righteous settlement. Such commitment meant he displayed little concern at suffering wounds himself, although with the close-quarter fighting of the day he was undeniably lucky to avoid any major injuries. Alan Marshall, a recent writer on Cromwell the soldier, believes his powers as a commander peaked at around 1644–5. 'The ideas of the Captain and Colonel of Horse in 1644–5 were in some ways the same ideas that he tried to exploit in 1648, 1649, 1650 and 1651, fast, mobile, dynamic and very aggressive warfare in campaigns of annihilation.'[23] If true, Cromwell would not be the first commander to form his main ideas as a relatively junior officer and, if no great innovator of war, by the time of Dunbar his army was well tried, fed on repeated successes, its soldiers having rare confidence in their zealous leader.

General Charles Fleetwood, Lieutenant General of Horse and Cromwell's nominal Second in Command
In 1642, together with other young men from the Inns of Court, Charles Fleetwood joined the Parliamentary cause by enlisting as a trooper in the Life Guards of the Earl of Essex. By May 1643 he had risen to captain and had been wounded at the first Battle of Newbury, following which his legal background led him to be given extra military responsibilities, namely seizing assets from sequestered Royalists in the eastern counties, for which he was rewarded with the Court of Wards, previously held by his father and his Royalist elder brother.[24]

Fleetwood went on to command a cavalry regiment in the Eastern Association which soon became noted for its large proportion of Puritan sectaries, both officers and troopers, whom he encouraged. As a result he was given command of a regiment of horse in the New Model Army, which he led at Naseby and in other engagements until April 1646, when he was returned to Parliament. In 1647, together with Fairfax, Cromwell and Ireton, Fleetwood was involved in the clash between the army and Parliament and it was his soldiers who seized the king at Holdenby, thereby strengthening the army's hand. After the abolition of the Court of Wards Fleetwood was compensated with a payment of £2,250, and apparently retired from public life, not fighting in the Second Civil War, being absent from the king's trial and not accompanying Cromwell on his expedition to Ireland.

His appointment as lieutenant general of horse for Cromwell's invasion of Scotland probably owed much to the number of other experienced commanders who remained in Ireland. Although Fleetwood had shown himself to be a good enough soldier up to regimental level, his support for godly congregations within the army helped to explain such rapid promotion: highly popular with the sectary elements in the army, Fleetwood represented a strong if narrow-minded believer whom Cromwell saw as compliant and reliable.

After Dunbar and Worcester, where he performed well enough in favourable circumstances, Fleetwood became a member of the all-powerful Council of State. In November 1651 after the death of Ireton he married Cromwell's daughter Bridget and in 1652, when Lambert declined the post, Fleetwood became commander in chief in Ireland. There 'he showed himself a supporter of transportation for the native Irish and a bitter prosecutor of Catholic priests',[25] although he also appeared out of his depth in the confused national and political cross-currents there and relied on Cromwell's continued support to retain his position in that country. Back in England as second in command of the army, Fleetwood tended to support whatever faction appeared to be in the ascendant, which for those out of favour earned him the sobriquet of 'the Weeping Anabaptist', and even Cromwell acknowledged his indecisiveness by calling him a 'milk sop'.[26] An undoubted survivor, after the Restoration the one-time prominent republican (albeit one who had no direct involvement in the king's execution) was allowed to live on undisturbed, providing he took up no public appointment.

Whatever Fleetwood's cautiousness and limitations of character, at Dunbar he carried out Cromwell's instructions in moving the English forward formations up until responsibility for them passed over to Lambert. As a fellow believer and a popular general in the army, Cromwell probably also saw him as a useful foil against his two leading battlefield commanders, John Lambert and George Monck, whose roles at Dunbar would ultimately be far more decisive than that of Charles Fleetwood.

Major General John Lambert, Major General of Foot and Cromwell's operational Second in Command

John Lambert was undoubtedly the most influential of Cromwell's commanders and considered by his biographer Lucas Phillips to have had military skills as high or higher than his master's.[27] Born into a leading Yorkshire family, Lambert made an immediate impact on the military scene. He was handsome and brave, a charming and cultured man with none of the religious fanaticism of Fleetwood or Cromwell. On the other hand, Lambert was undoubtedly vain and status-seeking and, as Phillips has observed, 'Had his greater qualities – his physical and moral courage, his driving power, his tolerance and generosity – been balanced by some political acumen, and had he sought to emulate Cromwell otherwise than by imitating him, he might well, since he had an immense following in the army, have attained that high seat to which his ambition aspired.'[28] Lucas Phillips stopped short of saying it, but Lambert too sought the highest post in the land, whether as a titular commander in chief of both army and Parliament or even as some form of constitutional monarch.

As a young man Lambert married Frances, daughter of Sir William Lister. She was not only beautiful but had a vivid personality and, like Sarah Churchill later in the century, acted as the main spur to her husband's ambition, becoming at the same time an especial favourite of Cromwell, who referred to her as 'his jewel'.

At the outset of the Civil War Lambert joined the Parliamentary forces under Lord Fairfax. During the early exchanges he was said to have 'carried himself very bravely'[29] and to have proved a natural soldier, but like Cromwell, Lambert's career surged following the Battle of Marston Moor in 1642. There he was part of the Parliamentary cavalry under Sir Thomas Fairfax, who were defeated by the Royalist commander George Goring, although Fairfax, accompanied by Lambert and six remaining troops, subsequently cut his way through to Cromwell and Leslie on their army's opposite wing, following which the combined formations cut Goring's cavalry to pieces and destroyed the Royalist Duke of Newcastle's famed white-coated infantry.

After Marston Moor Lambert suffered from a bout of ill health and stayed in London with his wife, but in 1647 the dispute between the army and Parliament brought him to the fore as spokesman for the army's discontented officers, and he assisted Ireton in drawing up the radical 'Heads of Proposals', which, among other things, opted to hold parliaments once every two years and to redistribute parliamentary seats on a more equal basis, thereby hopefully laying a foundation for what he saw as 'the common rights and liberties of the people and an established peace'.[30]

In 1648 Lambert, a major general before his twenty-ninth birthday, accepted his most responsible military task so far in defending the north of England against a series of Royalist uprisings and, more dangerous still, against an invasion from Scotland by the Engager army of 18,000 men led by the Duke of Hamilton. With his 5,000 soldiers he conducted a brilliant defensive campaign until joined by Cromwell, when together they struck at Hamilton's army at Preston, destroying the Scottish forces and taking 10,000 prisoners in an action where the energy and military skills of both men proved remarkable. Lambert was subsequently named as one of the members of the court appointed to try Charles I, but like Fairfax and Fleetwood he took no part in the trial.

It was no surprise that in 1650 Cromwell should once again call upon Lambert to assist him in commanding 'perhaps the finest English army that has ever been put in the field'[31] for his arduous invasion of Scotland, where he faced an astute and experienced opponent who was fighting on his home ground. At the Battle of Dunbar John Lambert's contributions, his rapid appreciation of the ground, strong powers of leadership and grasp of the tactical opportunities,[32] where he redeployed the army in the most adverse conditions, were to prove of the greatest advantage. Lambert's military skills were also much in evidence during the next year at Inverkeithing[33] and Worcester. Following his success at Inverkeithing, Cromwell suggested to Speaker Lenthall that Lambert should be rewarded: 'the carriage of the Major General as in all other things so in this, is worthy of your taking notice of.'[34] The Commons thereupon voted lands in Scotland to Lambert to the value of £1,000 a year.

In the years following Worcester, Lambert and Cromwell grew apart. Lambert, the doctrinaire republican, could never fully accept Cromwell as a de facto monarch, even if his title of Lord Protector (Lambert had suggested Lord Governer) was chosen because it was much less permanent than that of King. But while the office was elective, rather than hereditary, Cromwell occupied the Palace of Whitehall like previous kings and was known as His Highness the Royal Protector, who when he governed did so with almost unbounded authority. On 24 June 1657 Parliament required all Cromwell's councillors and officials to sign an oath of fidelity, but Lambert, who, despite his differences with the Protector considered he had remained loyal, refused to sign. He was immediately deprived of all his offices and for the rest of the Protectorate lived quietly in retirement, taking no part in the military intrigues that, at Cromwell's death, led to the appointment of his son, Richard, as Lord Protector. Following Richard's fall, Lambert was restored to his earlier army commands but when, in late 1659, he attempted to oppose Monck, who favoured welcoming back the king, Lambert's troops melted away. He was imprisoned and after the Restoration remained in open custody for the final twenty-three years of his life.

Whatever Lambert's political naivety, his remarkable military successes with Cromwell at Preston, followed by his notable contributions at Dunbar and later at Inverkeithing and Worcester, confirmed his position as a soldier of the first rank during the Commonwealth period.

General George Monck

While officially no more than a brigade commander with special responsibility for the artillery, George Monck also played an important part in Cromwell's military initiatives at Dunbar. A Devonian, the second son of Sir Thomas Monck and Elizabeth, daughter of Sir George Smith, he had the royal blood of the Plantagenets in his veins. Unlike John Lambert, Monck was not handsome but his broad, strong features topped a stocky and durable frame, and there was no doubting his determination, for as early as 1625, after the under-sheriff of Devon had treacherously allowed his father to be arrested as he went to pay his respects to the king, young George attacked him with a cudgel. As a result he had to leave the country, joining Sir Richard Grenville's expedition to Cadiz before entering service with the Dutch. There he showed his bravery and became known both for his military efficiency and as a strict disciplinarian.

At the beginning of the Civil War he returned to England at thirty years of age and was sent by Charles I to Ireland as a major general to the king's Irish Brigade. Returning to England he was in Nantwich with the Royalist army at their defeat by Fairfax, where he was taken prisoner; arraigned by Parliament for high treason, he was imprisoned in the Tower of London for more than three years, where he suffered from great deprivation, despite the receipt of many inviting offers from Parliament 'if only he would engage in their cause.'[35] At the late stages of the war Monck agreed to serve Parliament if it could be in Ireland, fighting the rebels there rather than the king. In Ireland Monck made a temporary peace with the Catholic Irish leader, Owen Roe O'Neill, before O'Neill was forced to surrender at Dundalk on 17 July 1649. Monck returned to explain himself to the House of Commons, which utterly disapproved of his accommodation with the Catholic O'Neill although declaring their continued belief in his good faith.

Despite Monck's questionable loyalty, Cromwell recognized his determination together with his military attributes, and decided to take him on his 1650 military expedition to Scotland. At Dunbar Monck commanded a brigade of foot with distinction, although the claims of his biographer, Thomas Gumble, that he had taught Cromwell and the others the art of war at Dunbar were undoubtedly much exaggerated.[36] After Dunbar and Inverkeithing, Cromwell left Monck as commander in chief in Scotland where he distinguished himself, and in 1652 he showed his versatility as one of the three generals of the English fleet before, in 1654, again taking on command of the army in Scotland and restoring order. Throughout Cromwell's rule Monck and Cromwell were in accord, with Cromwell describing Monck to another of his officers as 'Your honest general, George Monck, who is a simple-hearted man.'[37] In fact, the stolid tobacco-chewing Monck was a far more complex individual than the Protector realized and after Cromwell's death and the fall of his son Richard, Monck became the major military figure in Britain, outfacing the out-and-out republican Lambert before moving with his troops down to London, where he eventually entered into direct communication with Charles II. Monck recommended to the king that he offer a general pardon and an indemnity guaranteeing all sales of land by the late authorities, and give a promise of preserving religious toleration – which the king largely followed.

On 25 May 1660 when the king landed at Dover, Monck met him with 'expressions of humility and devotion'.[38] The next day he was knighted and shortly afterwards made Duke of Albemarle, and was granted a pension of £700 a year together with the property of New Hall in Essex. To the end of his life Monck, the moderate presbyterian, remained the same shrewd, stolid and dependable man who was committed to his country, whether ruled by Cromwell or a king. With little of Lambert's imagination but infinitely more resolution than Fleetwood, he was as stalwart when taking on the sheriff who had wronged his father or when, as Cromwell's protégé, he faced superior numbers of Scots across the Brox Burn at Dunbar. The man who survived so many dangers could not, however, escape the sharp pen of Samuel Pepys, who wrote disparagingly of his dullness: 'The blockhead Albemarle hath strange luck to be loved, though he be the heaviest man in the country.'[39]

* * * *

The English were well served by their leaders at Dunbar: apart from Cromwell himself, Lambert and Monck would have held their own in any military fraternity, before or since, and Fleetwood also carried out his duties well enough. Most important in all three cases, and for that matter with the other brigade and regimental commanders, their loyalty to their commander in chief was unswerving.

Chapter 4

The Scottish Army and its Commanders

The Lord's hand now upon us, our divisions.
(Robert Baillie, *Letters and Journals*)

The Scottish army under its commander in chief, General David Leslie, experienced far greater problems over both recruiting and retaining its men than its English opponent. From a small standing force of 2,500 cavalry and 3,000 foot at the beginning of 1650 it was decided to create an army of 19,000 by levy from the nation's pool of fit men. Because of earlier calls for levies the first Act did not prove fully effective and further legislation had to be passed, on 24 June and 3 July, to reach the original target and go on to raise larger numbers still.[1] Unlike the good proportion of experienced soldiers who rallied to join Cromwell on his invasion of Scotland, the vast majority of Scottish soldiers were either conscripts or men serving their clan leaders as they had from early medieval times, although a nucleus[2] from the army disbanded in 1647 remained, together with a number of ageing mercenaries from the earlier wars on the continent. A full call-out of men between sixteen and sixty was, of course, impractical, since not all were fit enough to be soldiers and such numbers would have been unmanageably large. In any case, farms and virtually all other undertakings needed men to help run them.

In practice, recruitment was carried out by each county sheriffdom in Scotland who appointed a shire committee of war, answerable to the central parliamentary Committee of Estates, to decide what proportion of its manpower could be levied. The repeated demands for men since 1638 and the serious wastage that had occurred over those years meant that raising a further army of 20,000 or more was neither a quick nor an easy process. In any case, for various reasons the responses from the counties tended to be uneven; in some areas, such as traditionally Royalist Aberdeenshire, the prospects of them providing many levies for an extreme Covenanting ministry (whether allegedly with Charles on its side or not) were unpromising. As a result the Scottish infantry regiments for the Dunbar campaign tended to be smaller and therefore more numerous, and with more colonels commanding them than their English counterparts.[3]

education possessing a great military genius and raising himself in the profession of arms'.[29] There was no doubt about his success in assembling the Scottish army, for as the shrewd religious commentator, Robert Baillie, acknowledged, 'We were feared that emulation among our Nobles might have done harm when they should be met in the field; but such was the wisdom of that old, little, crooked soldier, that all with an incredible submission from the beginning to the end, gave over themselves to be guided by him as if he had been the Great Solyman.'[30]

The unity and discipline that Leslie established in his Scottish army brought him speedy dividends and indeed set a standard for future Scottish commanders. His threat to the Newcastle coalfields resulted in the Scottish and English commissioners meeting at Ripon to work out a peace treaty, which agreed that Leslie's army should remain in Northumberland – indeed, England paid £250,000 sterling to support an army that Scotland had raised on its own behalf.

In 1641, following the so-called Second Bishops' War, Charles I realized that he had to treat with the Covenanters. Prior to entering Scotland he inspected their army at Newcastle, where he was lavishly entertained by Leslie, whom he agreed to make Earl of Leven on the tacit understanding that Leven would not again raise arms against him. A week later the army marched back into Scotland and was disbanded except for three regiments. Leven's biographer has observed that 'the old soldier stood in rather the same [dominant] situation to the King in Scotland as Cromwell stood in England after the founding of the New Model Army'.[31] But at this point the comparison ceased: whereas Cromwell was able to use his military power to have the king executed and to replace him as head of state, Leven, much the older man, had very different and far lower ambitions. Ever the pragmatist, he was fully aware that he could not satisfy both Charles I and the Covenanters and that his survival – together with that of his recently ennobled family – lay in faithfully serving his native country, which to him meant a Covenanting Scotland.

In 1642 Charles I ordered Leven to suppress a rising in Ulster by the Catholic Irish. It was his first and last military assignment on behalf of the king, for with the approach of the English Civil War and just prior to the English Parliament ratifying the Scottish League and Covenant, he was duly invited in August to assemble a Scottish army in support of the Parliamentarians. As the senior commander at Marston Moor he was in overall command of the allied forces, numbering 28,000 men, and it was his decision to make a surprise attack on the Royalists at about 7.30 p.m. on 2 July 1644. In the confused fighting Leven (who had earlier given ample evidence of his bravery in Europe) thought his side had lost and, together with the old Lord Fairfax, fled from the field, hardly drawing rein until he reached Leeds twenty-four miles away. But in fact the allies had won and although both Fairfax and Leven survived the crisis, from then onward it was Cromwell's military reputation that grew and Leven's that was in steady decline.

During 1645 his priority was to protect his native Scotland rather than clear the Royalist forces from the north of England, for in detaching Leslie's cavalry to deal with Montrose his army's ability to manoeuvre was seriously reduced. When

Charles I sought refuge in Leven's camp near Newark the Scottish commander made him a prisoner and after the army withdrew to Newcastle the severest pressure was put upon the king to accept the Covenant, but to no avail. With the Scots' hopes failing of getting the League and Covenant genuinely accepted outside Scotland, their attention turned to obtaining compensation for their expenses incurred in raising the army, which was itself suffering from a dire want of supplies of all kinds. The initial figure discussed was £1.8 million which was reduced to £400,000, of which only £200,000 was to be paid straightaway and only if they handed over Charles I to the English Parliament. On its return to Scotland Leven's army immediately began disbanding, and was eventually reduced to seven regiments of foot and 1,200 horse and dragoons, in Scotland's version of the New Model Army.

By this time Leven had become alarmed at the new feeling in Scotland in support of Charles I, and it was against his wishes that he was kept on as titular commander in chief of the reduced forces with David Leslie in charge of the army's operational responsibilities. Leven (like Leslie) refused outright to join in raising another Scottish army for the Engagers and their decision no doubt was also affected by the military difficulties of moving into England against Cromwell and his forces. After Cromwell destroyed the Engagers' army, Leven entertained him to dinner in Edinburgh Castle,[32] where it was agreed the Scottish forces should again be disbanded, except for a body of 500 men under Leven's command, but after the king's execution and Scotland's recognition of his son as their king, a full-scale invasion of Scotland by Cromwell seemed merely a matter of time. Old as he was, Leven was the obvious candidate to raise another national army, although he was less anxious than ever to lead it against Cromwell. He tried to decline and, in fact, laid down his baton before Parliament – but his resignation was refused since the Estates were reluctant to lose his experience entirely, and they assured Leven that with David Leslie there to assume the active command he would not be asked to do more than he could undertake.[33]

The presence of both David Leslie and the self-seeking Leven on the Dunbar campaign provokes obvious questions regarding their respective roles. Of the writers, Stuart Reid goes furthest in thinking that, in fact, it was Leven who still made the important decisions but cites no fresh evidence for his assertion, and it seems most unlikely that, after the disastrous precedent of using joint commanders set by James IV at Flodden 130 years earlier, the Scots would have used a similar system at Dunbar. Leven's knowledge and experience would have been of great value to David Leslie's councils of war, and the old man's continuing influence was demonstrated when he threatened to lay down his commission (again) if Charles II's proposal to make a rash attack upon the English prior to Dunbar was to be taken up. In any case, Leven fully supported the 'scorched earth' measures that denied Cromwell supplies and provisions during his advance up to Edinburgh, although the thoroughness with which they were carried out, leaving women, children and old men half-starving, speaks more of Leslie than Leven. And before Edinburgh it was Leslie's direct actions that so frustrated and baffled the English commander.

If the Scots' high command appeared to talk at times with more than one voice it was likely to have been because of the undue influence exercised by the fanatical ministers who accompanied the army, rather than because of any continuing rivalry between Leslie and Leven. Although they were not particularly close, there is no record of enmity between them; both held the same religious beliefs and Leslie had loyally supported Leven when he was commander in chief. With Cromwell the common enemy they had ample reason to co-operate. In any case, after more than forty-five years of military service Leven had been most reluctant to take part in such a perilous campaign – hardly the behaviour of someone attempting to dominate the man who was made commander in chief. In his turn, after waiting so long for command, David Leslie would desire to make and be seen to be making his own decisions.

* * * *

David Leslie's other subordinate commanders owed their military experience to service in Europe or during the earlier civil wars, in which the nature of their religious beliefs was of central importance. This continued to be the case during the Dunbar campaign where differences of belief within the presbyterian brotherhood affected their attitudes not only to the war but to their commander in chief.

Major General Sir Robert Montgomerie was Leslie's senior cavalry commander at Dunbar. Like so many others of his generation, after studying at the University of Glasgow Robert Montgomerie commenced his soldiering as a mercenary in Europe, although in 1643 this fifth son of Alexander Montgomerie, 6th Earl of Eglinton, was selected by his father to be lieutenant colonel of the family's horse levied from Ayrshire, Lanarkshire and Renfrewshire to serve in the Covenanting army in support of the English Parliamentarians against Charles I. Fighting under his father, he was severely wounded in the arm at Marston Moor but he kept his regiment in order there, despite the destruction of the other cavalry units on the right wing.[34] In 1645 he served on Leslie's Philiphaugh campaign against Montrose, replacing his father as the regiment's colonel, and he subsequently helped Leslie clear the north of Scotland of the Royalist forces who had supported Montrose. Like Leven and Leslie he refused to join the army of the moderate presbyterian Engagers, for which he was penalized on 11 May 1648 by losing his troop of horse to his brother, Hugh.

It was not all loss, however, since he was subsequently promoted to major general for the forces supporting the Kirk party against the Engagers. When Cromwell visited Edinburgh and was met by Leven, Montgomerie was given a letter[35] authorizing him to receive 2,000 of the Scottish prisoners taken after the Engagers' defeat at Preston. There he aimed to sell Scots – although not those of his own stern religious persuasion – to the King of Spain for service in the Low Countries, which, however humiliating, would have undoubtedly been far better for them than rotting in the jails of the time. Although Cromwell was very much in favour of removing them from the country, negotiations to bring this about proved abortive.

During 1650 Major General Montgomerie's cavalry units played a prominent part in David Leslie's attempts to block Cromwell's invasion of Scotland. In the early hours of 31 July Montgomerie attempted a surprise attack on Cromwell's forces near Musselburgh, during which he beat Cromwell's guards and 'put a regiment of horse in some disorder',[36] although when Cromwell brought up reinforcements Montgomerie was himself forced to retreat towards Edinburgh.

There is no reason to believe that David Leslie was not well and faithfully served by his commander of horse at Dunbar. Coming from a distinguished military tradition, Montgomerie had already shown his daring and natural powers of leadership both in Europe and against Royalist forces in England and Scotland, and then in 1650 during the hostilities before Dunbar. Although the details of his contributions in the battle itself are unknown, or, as reports had it, whether he might have been among those who were delayed coming upon the field, there are no doubts about his fighting qualities. After surviving the battle he retired under David Leslie to beyond the Forth, until, under the joint command of Leslie and Charles II, his cavalry distinguished themselves at the Battle of Worcester. Taken prisoner after the battle, he was sent to the Tower of London, from which this indomitable man managed to escape and, after further captures and evasions crossed the Channel to Europe. At the Restoration Charles II appointed him Lord of the Bedchamber, but Montgomerie's unyielding presbyterian beliefs and unwillingness to compromise were not welcome in such a libertarian court, with the result that he lost the king's favour and was imprisoned until 1668.

Lieutenant General Sir James Lumsden of Innergellie, Leslie's senior infantry commander at Dunbar, was the son of Robert Lumsden. His was a military family and two of his brothers, Robert and William, also became army officers.

In 1629 he was an ensign in Colonel James Spens's regiment serving King Gustavus Adolphus of Sweden, and by 1631 he was promoted to colonel; his contemporary, Colonel Robert Monro (much of whose later service was in Ireland), recalled them both leading their pikemen into Frankfurt. Lumsden later went on to distinguish himself further at the Battle of Leipzig in September 1631.

While commandant at Osnabruck in 1639 Lumsden asked to be released so that he might return to Scotland 'in order to safeguard not only his property but his honour',[37] which request was finally granted in August 1640. But so highly was he regarded by the Swedish royal family that, together with Alexander Leslie, Lumsden received a pension for life, a gold chain bearing Queen Christina's image, and 200 muskets and 200 suits of armour. He served in Alexander Leslie's Covenanting army which supported the English Parliamentarians and in 1643–4 acted as lieutenant colonel of Lord Gordon's Foot, which in 1644 became Lumsden's Foot. Lumsden accompanied Lord Fairfax's troops at the siege of York in June 1644 and drew up the plan for the Battle of Marston Moor (which is still in existence), where he commanded the Scottish foot that successfully supported the first-line infantry.

Lumsden was made governor of Newcastle in November 1644 and on 30 January 1647 Leven permitted him to talk with Charles I, apparently the only officer serving in the Covenanting army who could be trusted to withstand the king's wiles; he was, in fact, knighted around this time. In February Lumsden's regiment, together with the best part of the army, was disbanded, but by 1650 he had been appointed lieutenant general for the Dunbar campaign and in August of that year the Scottish Chancellor, the Earl of Loudon, wrote to Charles II praising Lumsden's loyalty both to the Covenant and himself. At Dunbar Lumsden's brigade resisted the English until it was virtually destroyed, although it is probable that Lumsden was delayed in joining it. Along with his brother James he was taken prisoner and played no part in the Worcester campaign the following year, regaining his liberty in 1652.[38]

Colonel Archibald Strachan, second in command of the Scottish cavalry at Dunbar, was an energetic and determined cavalry leader who had distinguished himself with David Leslie in the fighting preceding Dunbar. His career exemplified the confused loyalties that helped disorder Scotland's military performance at this time. His former life had apparently been 'very lewd' before he became religious and 'inclined much in opinion towards the sectaries'. As a major he served with Cromwell fighting against his fellow countrymen at Preston in 1648 and took part in the negotiations between Cromwell and Argyll during September 1648, remaining with Cromwell until after Charles I's execution.[39]

After much consideration of his previous scandalous conduct, the commission of the Kirk allowed him to sign the Covenant on 14 March 1649, and subsequently allotted him a troop of horse with which he energetically and implacably opposed all Royalists, who presently supported Charles II, and the so-called Malignants and Engagers, who had supported his father. Leven tried to remove him as a trouble-making 'sectary' but the Kirk supported Strachan, who proved confident and fearless in fighting for what he saw as God's cause, whatever the odds stacked against him. In 1650 he said, 'If James Grahame land near this quarters [Inverness] he will suddenly be deceased. And there shall be no need of the levy of knaves to the work tho' they should be willing',[40] and when Montrose did land in the north of Scotland, Strachan justified his words. At Leslie's orders he advanced with 230 horse, 36 musketeers and 400 men of the Ross and Monro clans. However, much as he believed in the Lord's support, he proved quite willing to benefit from expert local advice given by Alexander Monro, which enabled him to trick Montrose into thinking he had only one troop of horse, whereupon he routed Montrose's larger force of 1,200 foot (mostly raw levies) and his 40 horse. This victory led Strachan to think that numbers were unimportant if the cause was just.

Strachan was given £1,000 sterling and a gold chain from the Scottish Parliament after his success against Montrose, and his illusion of himself as the instrument of God was further strengthened by the lucky chance when, although hit during the fight, the bullet was stopped by his belt and thick buff coat. The Kirk contributed 100,000 marks towards founding a regiment for him, which he reputedly made the best in the army. He saw action under Montgomerie at Musselburgh on 30 July 1650 and at Dunbar he undoubtedly fought well against Lambert. Afterwards he blamed the battle's loss on Leslie and refused to serve under him further, initiating instead a correspondence with Cromwell, to whom he was much less hostile than to Charles II and his supporters. In fact, it was Charles's fear that Strachan might seize him and hand him over to Cromwell that led him to flee from Perth in October 1650.

Strachan put his name to the Remonstrance that was drawn up at Dumfries in protest against fighting for the king unless he abandoned the Malignants and other godless associates, and when such men were brought in to help build a new national army for Scotland Strachan transferred his allegiance to Cromwell and was said to have brought about the surrender of Edinburgh Castle. He was excommunicated on 12 January 1651, declared a traitor in April and his goods were forfeited. Although Cromwell offered him a command he took the excommunication so much to heart that he soon sickened and died. But, whatever the hostile feelings of this tortured man to Leslie after Dunbar, Strachan appeared to have fought bravely enough during the course of the battle itself.

* * * *

Such disparity in the members of the Scottish high command meant they could never achieve the same unanimity of purpose at Dunbar as the English. Unlike Cromwell with his guaranteed Parliamentary support, the 1650 campaign was Leslie's first occasion as a senior field commander and the Scottish Parliament did not trust him to act alone. Even more important, Leslie had no final power over the religious ministers accompanying the army, who not only advocated purges at the cost of its military efficiency, but also involved themselves in its tactical decisions in a way impossible with Cromwell. There is no reason to believe that Leslie and his subordinate commanders were any less stringent in their use of the military rank structure and its codes of discipline than the English, but at moments of ultimate danger – which were only too likely when fighting Cromwell – such different centres of authority and the ferocious and contrary nature of their personal beliefs, spelled potential trouble.

Part II

Push of Pike

Chapter 5
Probing the Scottish Defences

> The impossibility of our forcing them to fight by their alternate squatting
> on the fenny grounds and skipping like young goats in the mountains.
>
> (Charles Fleetwood, 30 August 1650)

On 4 July 1650 the English Parliament officially adopted its Council of State's proposal to invade Scotland. Cromwell, lord general and commander in chief in place of the reluctant Thomas Fairfax, proceeded to select his commanders from men in whom he knew he could trust. Secure in the support of such natural fighting soldiers as Lambert and Monck, and with Charles Fleetwood, his future son-in-law, as his official deputy, the post of commissary general went to a second son-in-law, Edward Whalley, former woollen draper and regicide. Among his colonels were officers such as Thomas Pride, Robert Lilburne, John Okey and Whalley's own son-in-law, William Goffe. At the same time, since the rank and file for his invading army had enlisted a month before and were by now at Newcastle, Cromwell endeavoured to protect his back by putting Thomas Harrison, another regicide from humble beginnings, in charge of the troops that remained in the south of England. With a complement of 17,000 it was a relatively small army, with limited numbers of baggage wagons, for the formidable task of defeating the Scottish forces, ending Scottish support for Charles II and installing an English garrison in that country, but to balance that, its veteran soldiers were commanded by experienced officers well known to their men. In any case, the English Parliament had agreed to send Cromwell a further 8,500 men when they could be made available. According to Robert Baillie, Cromwell was so satisfied with his army's original complement that he had already assured 'his brethren in evil of a more easy conquest of that kingdom [Scotland] than all the English kings ever had'.[1]

In Scotland the arrangements for defence being made by the dominant Kirk party under Archibald Campbell, Marquis of Argyll, included raising a considerably larger army. The Covenanters brooked no opposition and, in the case of civilians with differing religious or political convictions, were prepared to award such savage punishments as 'scourging, the nailing of lugs (ears) and boring of tongues'.[2] To bring their army to unquestioning obedience they not only aimed to remove any Engagers who had supported Charles I but also tried to keep his young and personable successor, Charles II, from any contact with the soldiers. It was thus that with the new king excluded and Leven, Scotland's veteran military leader, too old, David Leslie had assumed the active command.

While Cromwell justified his invasion of Scotland to the English Council of State by citing a likely Scottish attack upon England, Leslie's defensive stance centred upon his attempts to make the Scottish capital, together with its port of Leith, invincible by building a strong defensive box running from the port to the city and its castle. He endeavoured to make the invading army's task more difficult still by removing all active males between the ages of seven and seventy from the eastern region of Scotland (stretching northward from Berwick right up to Edinburgh), including the Lammermuir Hills covering the more central approaches to the capital. Leslie had all the cattle and sheep driven north of the Forth, the corn harvested and carted away, and he appropriated any stocks of food there, even confiscating griddles and other such implements which the English might use to prepare their meals. Infirm men, wives and children were left to face the English soldiers. Cromwell's Captain Hodgson, for instance, described such women at Dunbar as 'pitiful, sorry creatures, clothed in white flannell in a very homely manner',[3] although the English succeeded in persuading some to bake and brew for them, doubtless in exchange for promises of food arriving by sea.

During Cromwell's move north he was entertained by civic officials at Northampton, Leicester and York, before continuing to Durham where he was greeted by the governor of Newcastle, Sir Arthur Hesilrige, accompanied by Cromwell's regimental colonels. After his experience in Ireland, he no doubt appreciated such civic courtesies, although at Durham Cromwell quickly became more aware of the nature and thoroughness of the Scottish preparations. By 10 July he had reached Newcastle where he made an initial inspection of the army: many of the soldiers had already served with him and he was able to greet some by name and to dismiss any dissentients like Colonel Bright who, along with several more junior officers, considered any invasion of Scotland unjustifiable. At Newcastle Cromwell also took the opportunity of giving his two favoured commanders, Lambert and Monck, direct regimental responsibilities in addition to the command roles he had planned for them.

As in Ireland, Cromwell had already instigated a blockade of the Scottish ports, for, by gaining control of the country's coastal waters, he planned to insulate his army from the problems of crossing the barren, stripped countryside of southern Scotland by supplying it from the sea. Twenty-three ships were hired in July for this purpose but, with their capacity falling short of the totals required, during August the Council of State ordered the admiralty to hire as many as it wanted, following which the total rose to 140. These were scheduled to deliver no less than 2,800 tons of oats and 10,700 tons of hay, among other supplies, to designated ports on the Scottish east coast.[4]

Cromwell undoubtedly needed to keep his army in good shape for an anticipated encounter against superior numbers. But whatever the strength of Scottish martial traditions, after his previous successes against the Engagers, Cromwell was confident of defeating them again. He also reasoned that through their marching and bivouacking together during the sixty-mile journey from Newcastle to Berwick, his regiments would regain their renowned *esprit de corps* and if the Scots made any unlikely attempt to block their progress, so much the better. Whatever their morale, one observer said they quickly became excellent cooks, even using their back plates as dripping pans and their headpieces for boiling porridge.[5] Cromwell made no attempt to hurry and after nine days' steady marching he held a grand review at Chillingham Castle, outside Berwick, to boost his army's morale still further.

By this time he had commenced a war of words to exploit the strained loyalties currently within Scotland, inviting individuals opposed to the Kirk party to join him, while his army was still being reviewed at Chillingham Castle. The secretary of the army, John Rushworth, sent out the following appeal to the people of Scotland: 'Declaration of the Army of England upon their march into Scotland to all that are Saints and partakers of the Faith of God's elect in Scotland. That in Charles Stuart and his party there can be no Salvation; that we seek the real substance of the Covenant; that it goes against our heart to hurt a hair of any sincere servant of God.'[6] Cromwell and others of his officers had spent a considerable time drafting it; an effort they considered worthwhile for, unlike the heretic Irish, the Scots were part of the Protestant fraternity, even if they were deluded in their support for Charles II and by thinking that presbyterianism should be adopted by all the home countries.

In the Scottish camp David Leslie, who previously had tended to favour quick and decisive battlefield moves, also adopted a different strategy, as well as embarking on his own version of psychological warfare. He had little option, for with the country's protracted system of mobilization his army was not yet at full strength, and by 21 June his problems had been compounded when the Kirk party set up a committee to purge it of unsuitable members. In the circumstances he needed as long as possible to ready his forces and to construct truly formidable defences around Edinburgh. In the meanwhile anything that helped him blunt Cromwell's military threat was welcome. In this regard he had the Kirk's ministers send messages to their congregations in southern Scotland predicting the same savagery from the English soldiers that had befallen the Irish, not only laying waste to the land but putting 'all men to the sword and to thrust hot irons through the women's breasts'.[7] The veteran Ironside, Captain Hodgson, drily observed, 'The clergy highly incensed against us represent us to the people as if we had been the monsters of the world.'[8]

This caused Cromwell to draw up a stern proclamation which, preceded by the customary trumpet calls and drum roll, was read out to all his parading regiments, threatening with death any soldier guilty of violent conduct or plundering. Cromwell also took pains to assure the inhabitants of southern Scotland of his protection, and when his cavalry took a few early prisoners he was careful to demonstrate his clemency by allowing them to return home on condition they would not bear arms against him in the future.

After such verbal exchanges, action was resumed when the English army crossed the border on 22 July, relatively late in the campaigning season. Prior to this Cromwell issued another proclamation to his soldiers explaining the grounds of the present expedition 'in relation to his coming over from Ireland',[9] in which he enjoined his officers to 'double, nay treble, their diligence in that place for be sure we had work before us'.[10] These words were greeted with loud acclamations, and then, with Cromwell's and Pride's regiments leading, the army ceremonially stepped onto Scottish soil. At Ayton, four miles into Scotland, they halted in the hope of tempting the Scottish forces into disputing their progress, but meeting with no opposition they advanced a further twelve miles to Cockburnspath where about six miles east of Dunbar there was 'a wild rock – and river – chasm, through which the great road goes.'[11] They probably encamped on the flat ground close to the walls of Cockburnspath Tower. If the Scots had wanted to make any sort of a stand this would have been an obvious place, but the English march remained undisputed.

Since entering Scotland the weather had been unsettled, as it was throughout that summer, and the army lived 'with hard accommodation out of doors'.[12] This meant sleeping in the open (tents had not yet been supplied) and subsisting in the main on a diet of (stale) biscuit and cheese, for they were unable to acquire any additional food supplies or heating materials from the local population. A former English army under Edward II, which went on to meet Robert Bruce at Bannockburn and suffer a crushing defeat there, had experienced similar difficulties from the 'scorched earth' measures adopted by their opponents, although in 1650 the English organization and leadership were undoubtedly superior. In any case, the lack of opposition so far probably came as no surprise to the English leader, for he had placed a spy in Edinburgh who reported on many matters, including the extent of the work on the city's defences, to Cromwell's Newcastle agent, William Rowe.

On 26 July the English resumed their progress along the coast road and reached Dunbar, where they found adverse winds had delayed many of the supply ships and the totals of food awaiting them were described as no more than a 'small pittance'. On the next day, in the customary pouring rain they set off inland on an eleven-mile march that took them through the village of East Linton, with its strong castle, to Haddington. They were now just twelve miles from Edinburgh, with Leslie's forward outposts at Gladsmuir less than half that distance away. English hopes of precipitating a battle rose but when, on Sunday 28 July, Cromwell sent out a strong cavalry force under Lambert and Whalley, the opposing Scottish horsemen took off, thus marking Leslie's campaign tactics. Lambert pressed on to occupy the small port of Musselburgh three miles from Leslie's main defensive positions and the rest of the army followed, but disappointingly for them Musselburgh's open sandy beaches were hardly ideal for supply ships. Although flat-bottomed ones could be beached and unloaded directly or small craft used to bring their contents off, in bad weather neither method could be relied on.

However vigilant Cromwell had urged his men to be, during their eight days since crossing the border and moving through a desolate and sodden countryside

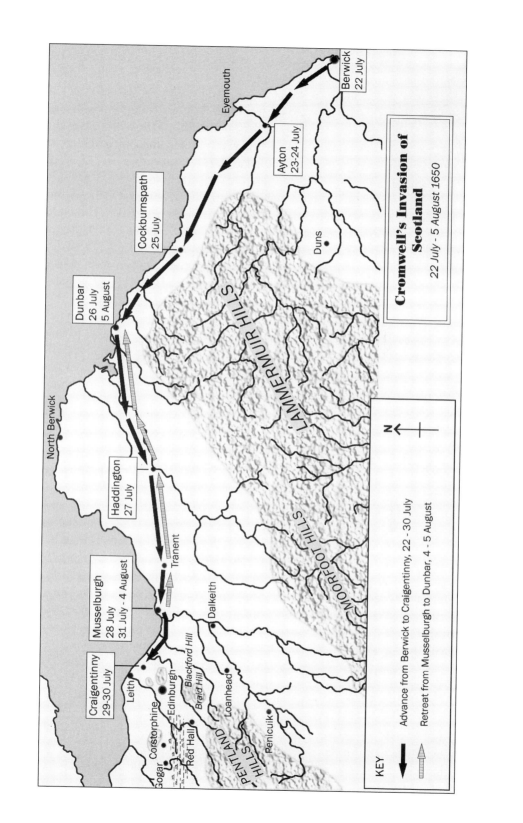

Cromwell's Invasion of Scotland
22 July - 5 August 1650

Berwick
22 July

Ayton
23-24 July

Cockburnspath
25 July

Dunbar
26 July
5 August

Haddington
27 July

Musselburgh
28 July
31 July - 4 August

Craigentinny
29-30 July

Eyemouth

Duns

North Berwick

Tranent

Dalkeith

Leith

Edinburgh

Corstorphine

Gogar

Red Hall

Blackford Hill

Braid Hill

Loanhead

Penicuik

LAMMERMUIR HILLS

MOORFOOT HILLS

PENTLAND HILLS

N

KEY

Advance from Berwick to Craigentinny, 22 - 30 July

Retreat from Musselburgh to Dunbar, 4 - 5 August

they had met with virtually no resistance, although this had not prevented it from being a taxing journey; with the effects of the adverse weather exacerbated by the army's lack of tents and its shortage of food. As a result the dysentery that had previously afflicted Cromwell's soldiers in Ireland resurfaced, although widespread suspicions were voiced against the local small beer 'which hath such a filthy tange and so laxative that it brought the flux'.[13] Such complaints, typical of good and bad soldiers alike, could only be expected to cease if they succeeded in coming to grips with the Scottish army.

On 29 July they attempted to do so. Leaving Musselburgh they moved forward onto the flat ground directly before the Scots' positions near the coast, where a hundred years before the English had defeated a Scottish army at the Battle of Pinkie, largely as a result of the artillery support given by their seaborne guns.

This time Leslie showed no intention of fighting on the open plain. Despite his superior numbers, Cromwell's reputation, together with the variable military experience of his own men and the continuing interference he was suffering from the Kirk, led him to believe he could use the strength of his defences to greater effect. Why risk fighting in the open when the English could waste their strength against them? In fact, he had already made good use of Edinburgh's natural features, placing an outpost on the hill called Arthur's Seat overlooking Holyrood House, with other advance guards on St Leonard's Crags and Blackford Hill further to the south and west. Such outposts were also designed to help obstruct an invading army if it began to move round the south of Edinburgh. By far the most notable of his man-made defences was a multiple line of trenches, in front of which spears were embedded in the ground to counteract charges from cavalry. These ran from the port of Leith in the north (whose sea approaches were blocked by a large 'boome' and whose strengthened walls carried forty guns) along the path of the present Leith Walk to Holyrood House and Abbey Hill, from where the city walls turned westward and joined the castle's fortifications. Other trenches on Calton Hill gave further protection to his defensive complex.

To the English commanders Scotland would already have seemed a much harder nut to crack than Ireland. Unlike the Irish, the Scots were prepared to leave their subsidiary ports open to the invaders and concentrate on defending their capital, which, elevated on the city's granite outcrop, presented a massive challenge for Cromwell's artillery, whose numbers were too few to mount a major siege. He could conceivably – at some considerable cost to his men – have created a breach in Leslie's eastern trench defences, but enlarging it against a determined enemy was likely to have brought many more casualties, with no guarantee that Leslie, like the Irish commander Hugh O'Neill at Clonmel earlier in the year, would not shut off the bridgehead by constructing a second or even a third defence line.

Possibly with Clonmel in mind, Cromwell rejected a frontal assault, preferring to goad Leslie into making a serious error. He began by sending a mixed party of musketeers and horse to occupy Arthur's Seat overlooking the southernmost area of the town. Having driven off the Scottish detachment there, he had Monck drag up two field pieces to fire upon the Scottish defence lines while, at the same time, four ships, the *Liberty*, the *Heart*, the *Garland* and the *Dolphin*, commanded by Captain Hall, cannonaded the port of Leith with fireballs and other missiles. In reply a Scottish force led by Colonel James Campbell of Lawers retook Arthur's Seat and captured the two cannon, only to be driven off it almost immediately with the loss of some men. Such 'huffing and puffing' by Cromwell on the edge of the Scottish defences and his positioning of just two guns on Arthur's Seat with which to bombard the Scots predictably failed to move them out of their trenches and scarcely furthered his object of gaining the port of Leith, although at one point the dashing Lambert led his cavalry up to the lip of the Scottish positions. Even so, in making this attempt the English were in the open for a full day and the following night under torrential rain. Cromwell acknowledged it was 'so sore a day and night of rain as I have seldom seen and greatly to our disadvantage'.[14] Following a council of war held the following morning, orders were given for the already 'tired, weary and dirtied' army to fall back to Musselburgh (and possibly Dunbar) where they could be given food and shelter and await a more favourable 'opportunity for adopting severer and more effective measures against the Scots'.[15]

Responsibility for covering the retreat went to the tireless Lambert, who had already much distinguished himself and who needed to remain vigilant, for David Leslie was not prepared to allow the tired and dispirited English an easy passage back. A series of running fights between the cavalry of both sides followed. Leslie sent out two detachments, one from Leith and the other from the Canongate further south, to deliver a pincer movement on the English rearguard, which during the army's retreat had become separated; the former was quickly driven off by Colonel Hacker's regiment, but the southern thrust succeeded in surrounding Captain Evanson and his 200 troopers. They were saved by a strike from Cromwell's own regiment, which drove off the attackers only for it to come under attack from other Scottish horse which, in turn, were set upon by Lambert's and Whalley's combined regiments. During this fast-moving encounter Lambert had his horse killed under him and after being wounded in the thigh and with his shoulder run through with a lance, he was snatched by the Scots before being rescued immediately by Lieutenant Empson, supported by six troopers from Hacker's regiment. The English had come within an ace of losing their best commander and Cromwell rapidly promoted Empson to captain, in spite of his reputation of being a better preacher than fighting soldier.[16]

After beating off the Scottish attacks the English continued towards Musselburgh, but on their arrival they found that about 500 of the local population (who had been hiding in the nearby coal pits) had returned to barricade the town. Lambert's cavalry, under Major Haines, were given the task of retaking it, which they did swiftly and effectively, killing thirty or more defenders in the process. The Scots, however, refused to submit, and that night presented the English with another and much more serious challenge. Leslie ordered a powerful force, of between 800 and 1,500 horse, under Major General Montgomerie accompanied by Colonels Lockhart, Strachan and

Ker, to attack the English lines and attempt to capture Cromwell himself. Despite Montgomerie's known hatred of Royalists, English Cavaliers loyal to Charles II and others who had already proved their worth in the field, however suspect their religious views, were allowed to ride with them. At 3 a.m., in pouring rain, they approached an English forward post manned by Lilburne's regiment. The alarm was raised, but two Englishmen in the Scottish party went forward and in English accents called out that it was a false alarm. Having deceived the guards, they scattered the opposition and made their way to Musselburgh, where they defeated a unit from Fleetwood's regiment before being themselves galled by a volley from Lambert's musketeers, whereupon additional troopers from Lilburne's reserve arrived and succeeded in driving them out. During the engagement, which brought the English army another near sleepless night, forty or fifty Scots were killed and several officers, together with eighty troopers, were captured.

Nonetheless, Cromwell's probing attacks had failed to bring out the Scottish main army, and during the engagements between the opposed cavalry detachments the lighter Scots horse had been led with skill and determination, although Cromwell was correct when he reported to the English Council of State that his heavier cavalry generally had the best of things: 'this is a sweet beginning of your business, or rather the Lord's; and I believe is not very satisfactory to the enemy, especially to the Kirk party.'[17] He also assured them his casualties were minimal – 'but a cornet; I do not hear of four men more' – although at the same time he acknowledged the main problems he presently faced were logistical: 'we shall famish for want of provisions if we be not timely and fully supplied.'[18] Cromwell's assessment was well founded, for not only had the defence lines proved too strong but up to this time the harbour at Musselburgh had been unable to unload anything like the supplies needed, thus making his army's return on 5 August to the all-weather, if small, port of Dunbar inevitable.

In the meanwhile, Cromwell maintained his psychological offensive by treating the Scottish wounded with notable kindness, even sending them back to Edinburgh in his coach, and releasing other prisoners on parole. He also wrote to Leslie and the Kirk's General Assembly, roundly accusing them of blind prejudice: 'Your own guilt is too much for you to bear: bring not therefore upon yourselves the blood of innocent men, – deceived with pretences of King and Covenant – I beseech you, in the bowels of Christ, think it possible you may be mistaken.' Cromwell followed this with an open threat: 'there may be a Covenant made with Death and Hell! Bethink yourselves.'[19] Such 'carrot and stick' approaches might have seemed necessary for Cromwell since his army appeared too weak to storm a fortified Edinburgh and, whatever quantities of food he could land, his limited number of carts prevented him from besieging the Scottish capital for long. Nonetheless, with such Covenanting ministers the chances of them admitting they were wrong to an arch-independent like Oliver Cromwell seemed negligible.

In the Scottish camp Leslie had serious military problems of his own: his defensive stance was unpopular with both the hot-blooded among his soldiers and his extreme

Covenanting ministers. The latter asked why godly, like-minded troops going about God's business, such as those who had been led successfully by Colonel Strachan against Montrose's superior numbers (of raw troops) at Carbisdale, should not carry the day against superior numbers of Cromwell's wrong-thinking sectaries. The initial successes of Montgomerie and Strachan at Musselburgh had also provoked the Kirk party, especially the fanatical and influential Archibald Wariston, into thinking that if Leslie had only used 1,500 troopers rather than 800 they would have been victorious.

Another threat to the continuity of Leslie's military plans came from Charles II, who on 29 July went to Leith to be greeted enthusiastically by the army, where his presence helped to fuel the militant spirit shown in pursuing the English to Musselburgh. For such men as Wariston, to whom it was essential that the Kirk party – not the Royalists – should vanquish Cromwell, this was appalling; indeed it was doubtful whether Wariston saw Charles II rather than Cromwell as the greater enemy. As a result, the king was rebutted and between 2 and 5 August the Kirk's purging committee resumed its activities against Leslie's army, removing another 3,000 soldiers and 80 officers for being insufficiently godly (in the Kirk's especial sense) at the very time he was trying to build a sense of cohesion and loyalty within it. With so much turbulence in the Scottish camp the timing of Cromwell's letter to the Scottish Kirk concerning their unreasoning prejudice was entirely relevant.

The English stayed at Dunbar from 5 to 10 August, recovering their condition, before Cromwell made another attempt to bring Leslie to battle prior to the approach of autumn, when campaigning would be even more difficult. His supply ships had recently been getting through to the port and he was able to issue each soldier with three days' rations of bread and cheese, before moving forward again to Musselburgh. In fact Cromwell even had spare rations, and he was able to safeguard his base by issuing corn and peas to its townspeople.

While at Dunbar, the English high command were sure to have discussed their tactical options. They could, of course, stay where they were and wait for Leslie to make the first move, but it was extremely unlikely he would risk leaving the security of Edinburgh and, in any case one could never imagine Cromwell surrendering the initiative in this way; they could mount a direct attack on Leslie's fortifications on the city's eastern side (a course of action strongly opposed by George Monck and others); or, with Leslie experiencing major difficulties in provisioning his own army, they could carry out an outflanking march round the west of Leslie's strong points, thereby threatening his food supplies from the fertile plain lying between Edinburgh and Glasgow. This march could conceivably continue to Queensferry on the Forth where it was hoped the English would be able to meet up with their fleet and also cut off Leslie's communications with the north of Scotland. With its supply lines cut, the Scottish army would be obliged either to give battle or to relinquish Edinburgh to the English. The latter option was adopted, and on 12 August Cromwell led his army back to its previous starting point at Musselburgh and Inveresk.

In the meantime attempts had been undertaken by both sides to strengthen their forces. The English commissioned four extra troops of dragoons to safeguard

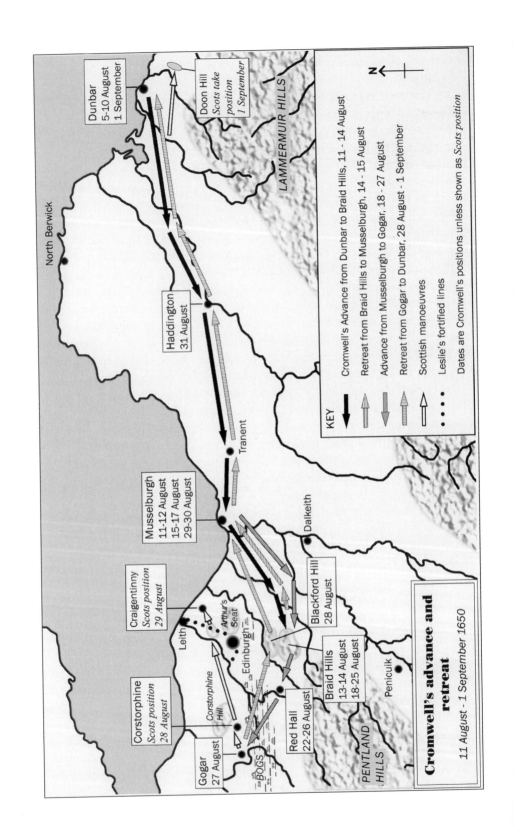

North Berwick

Dunbar
5-10 August
1 September

Doon Hill
*Scots take
position
1 September*

LAMMERMUIR HILLS

Haddington
31 August

Tranent

Musselburgh
11-12 August
15-17 August
29-30 August

Craigentinny
*Scots position
29 August*

Dalkeith

Leith

Arthur's
Seat

Blackford Hill
28 August

Corstorphine
*Scots position
28 August*

Corstorphine
Hill

Edinburgh

Braid Hills
13-14 August
18-25 August

Penicuik

Gogar
27 August

BOGS

Red Hall
22-26 August

PENTLAND
HILLS

KEY

→ Cromwell's Advance from Dunbar to Braid Hills, 11 - 14 August

⇑ Retreat from Braid Hills to Musselburgh, 14 - 15 August

⇓ Advance from Musselburgh to Gogar, 18 - 27 August

⇑ Retreat from Gogar to Dunbar, 28 August - 1 September

⇧ Scottish manoeuvres

···· Leslie's fortified lines

Dates are Cromwell's positions unless shown as *Scots position*

N

Cromwell's advance and retreat

11 August - 1 September 1650

Cromwell's seaward communications with Berwick, while Newcastle's governor, Sir Arthur Hesilrige, had been commanded to raise a regiment of horse and two of foot to help prevent 'irruptions' by the Scots against the English land supply lines. The Scottish initiatives were less straightforward, although Leslie's order for the recruits currently being gathered in the Highlands to march directly to Edinburgh, rather than muster at Perth under the king, promised to give his numbers a significant boost.

The Ironsides left Musselburgh on Sunday 13 August and following a feinting move, made camp in the Braid Hills south of the city, from where Cromwell attempted to foster a rift between the strong supporters of the Kirk party and those who were likely to be influenced by the rising fortunes of the young king, by despatching a personal appeal to Leslie for negotiation. This met with no apparent success, although on the open sands outside Leith selected English officers escorted by 100 troopers met a group of Scottish officers similarly protected. Why Leslie allowed such a meeting is not clear, for all the likely benefits lay with Cromwell, who hoped that strong Covenanter officers, such as Strachan and Ker, would desert. Nothing tangible appeared to come from the meeting, although it could only have put additional strains upon the ravelled Scottish loyalties at that time.

Cromwell's forward move did not provoke Leslie into risking battle. Still lacking sufficient carts, on 15 August Cromwell had his troops march back the eight miles to Musselburgh to pick up more food, together with their much needed tents, before returning three days later to re-encamp in the Braid Hills just south of Arthur's Seat, where they pitched their tents 'on a piece of ground pretty secure'[20] and awaited his orders.

From this location Cromwell had a number of possible moves round the city, the most likely being one further west, before turning north towards Queensferry. On his arrival Cromwell sent out skirmishers who captured a substantial building at Colinton, on his route to the Water of Leith, giving him another, if not particularly important, outpost round Edinburgh. Leslie responded by moving his army onto the strong feature of Corstophine Hill, protected from the south by two lochs.

The frustration felt at this point by Cromwell and his experienced commanders, with their army's laborious progress across wet and broken country intersected by deep watercourses, against an opponent with superior knowledge of the ground conditions, requires no emphasis. Leslie appeared to have got the better of them again, but by careful reconnaissance they might yet find a means of so menacing the Scottish western supply lines that their army would finally be driven into a stand-up fight.[21]

Cromwell took part in the reconnoitring and while he was thus engaged a Scottish dragoon fired an optimistic long shot at him. Cromwell laughed loudly at his inaccuracy, shouting out that if the soldier had been under his command he would have been punished, with the soldier's retort that he had, in fact, fought under Cromwell at Marston Moor illustrating the fast changing allegiances during the Civil War years.

The English reconnaissances were sure to have included the upper reaches of the Water of Leith, which they had to cross as they moved westward. This represented a major obstacle, for the valley cut by the river was like Cockburnspath in miniature, with steep rocky banks that were in places precipitous. Some idea of its hazardous nature can be gathered from Sir William Fraser, who likened it to the dizzy sheer pass at Killiecrankie.[22] Overlooking Slate Ford, the chosen crossing place for Cromwell's army, stood Red Hall, the baronial home of Sir James Hamilton. Its defences had long been neglected but Leslie had probably reinforced its garrison and, in any case, it held a commanding position upon the English line of march, whether they decided to move west or northward along the Leith valley towards Queensferry. Cromwell therefore ordered Red Hall's capture. This took two days to accomplish, during which field guns were brought up to mount a six-hour bombardment, before Monck's new regiment could storm the building. Despite the angry response of many in his army, Leslie refused to be drawn into a more general action,[23] although after its capture another meeting was held between English and Scottish officers, but again nothing seemed to come of it.[24]

With Red Hall safely in his hands, Cromwell resumed his march westward with Leslie shadowing him along the shorter route closer to Edinburgh. In fact, the Scottish army drew ahead and halted where the road to Glasgow crossed the Gogar Burn. Here they formed up in battalions on the open fields near Gogar Park and the hamlet of Gogar. The pursuing English had by far the more difficult journey: after the steep valley of Leith Water they had to cross the Murray Burn, followed by Gogar Burn with its crumbling banks, until they reached somewhat higher ground at Gogar Bank to the south of the Scottish positions. Here, seeing the Scottish army before them, they deployed for the long-awaited battle, and many of the English soldiers discarded their tents and any extra food likely to hinder them. Cromwell's scouts then discovered that Leslie's position was even stronger than his previous one on Corstophine Hill. Although the two armies were 'within less than twice musket-shot of each other', a loch and a treacherous swamp, which were not immediately discernible, extended right across the intervening ground. What with this forward obstacle and the 'wild, intricate, watery wilderness of bogs and quagmires',[25] together with the walls round Gogar House, covering the Scottish flanks, no attack was possible and both sides contented themselves with firing at each other with their artillery. They did so all day, firing several hundred rounds. The Scottish artillery positioned north of the burn near Gogar's present standing stone and the ruined policies at Hanley, brought into play several novel kinds of field pieces recently invented by their general of artillery, Colonel Wemyss.[26] Captain Hodgson was dismissive of them, saying that much of the shot flew over or fell short and the English artillery, positioned on the higher ground of Gogar Bank and Over Gogar, seemed to get rather the better of the exchanges. Cromwell reckoned the Scots' casualties were about eighty killed, including some of their considerable officers, with his own at no more than twenty, but not one commissioned officer.[27] Whether Cromwell's figures were accurate or not, for an army as large as the Scottish one their total casualties were still not significant. One memory of the exchange survives in the name of the locality, Gogar Flashes. Not only did the exchange see firearms of greater power and variety being used than was usual at that time, but the cannonade apparently went on until dusk.[28]

After Gogar the English faced yet another major obstacle to their north-westward move in the River Almond, and the extended exchange between the two sides' artillery at Gogar did in fact mark the end of Cromwell's attempts during August to take Edinburgh and defeat the Scottish army guarding it. The need to make laborious marches on short rations in the cold and wet when, against all expectations, their skilled and elusive opponent retained effective control of his army, caused Cromwell to blink first. With his alarming numbers of sick he realized he had to return to Musselburgh, if not Dunbar.

On 28 August, following a tempestuous night, dawn brought more rain and after renewing their cannonade for an hour or two, during the late morning the English commenced their eastward journey to Musselburgh. The Scots simultaneously moved back to Corstophine and it became a race between the two armies. As before, most of the advantages lay with the Scots, who occupied the interior lines of communication along with the higher ground, while Cromwell had to march along 'the soft, southern verge of those heart-breaking morasses'. It was hardly surprising, then, that even with such a veteran army and its famed leader, the frustrations of the last five weeks of campaigning should be affecting morale. One Ironside concluded that it was 'our lying there upon these cold hills brought sickness upon the souldiers, the flux and other sickness being (now) much among them',[29] and Captain John Hodgson even went so far as to call them 'a poor shattered, hungry, discouraged army'.[30]

The English removed their garrisons from Colinton and Red Hall and made camp on Blackford Hill, almost due south of the city and close to their former camp in the Braid Hills, with Leslie moving past them onto Calton Hill close to the Scots' previous defence lines to the east side of the city. Early on the 29th the English set off on their final leg for Musselburgh while preventing any interference from the Scots by keeping Duddingston Loch between the two armies. After crossing the bridge over the Magdalen Burn, they reached the port that same day, from where on the following day (the 30th) Cromwell sent off 500 of his sick – men unable to march any further – by ship to Berwick. Another council of war was held, where it was decided that 'with sickness and the wild weather coming on us, rendering even victual uncertain, and *no battle to be had* we clearly cannot continue here.'[31] Leslie had done his best to make Musselburgh unwelcoming by ordering out of their homes the Scots women who had previously baked and brewed for the English, and Cromwell realized he had no choice but to return once more to Dunbar with its all-weather harbour and ample caches of food, from where he could take stock and, possibly as a last resort, fortify the town and make it his winter quarters.

It was a bitter decision, for it acknowledged that for over five weeks, from 22 July to 31 August, since invading Scotland his formidable army had failed to bring their

Scottish opponents to battle or to cut off their supplies, despite the high physical demands of moving not only his infantry and cavalry but the artillery around Edinburgh's towering walls. His attempts to weaken the Kirk party's resolve through psychological measures had also failed. In contrast, Leslie had successfully exploited Scotland's traditional defences – its bad weather and remoteness (accentuated by his plundering of the land) – to bring the English to their knees. He had forced them to withdraw once and they were doing so again, while their numbers had fallen from 16,000 to 12,000, with the sickness still among them. There also appeared to be a greater finality about this second withdrawal, for the English fired their huts before they left.[32]

Through his leadership skills, David Leslie appeared to have given himself a genuine opportunity to move onto the offensive and even administer the *coup de grâce* against a faltering and much diminished English army. It was now a question of whether he had the courage and ability to strike such a blow and, if so, when and where?

Chapter 6

Back to Dunbar

> Our lying here daily consumeth our men, who fall sick beyond imagination.
>
> (Cromwell, *Letters*)

On Saturday 31 August the English army set off to march from Musselburgh to Haddington about eight miles away. In normal circumstances this was but a short day's journey, especially along a main road, but many of the soldiers were showing symptoms of the flux and after five weeks of continual wind and rain, while marching and counter-marching around Edinburgh, it was quite far enough. From Haddington they still faced a nine-mile journey to their base at Dunbar.

With Leslie in pursuit few Englishmen would have favoured the chance of their journey to Haddington going unimpeded, and as expected they were soon harried, first by the Scottish horse and then by the main army, to such a degree that by the end of the day Cromwell's own cavalry rearguard was in considerable danger. He described the situation to William Lenthall, the Speaker of the House of Commons, saying of the Scots: 'They had marched with that exceeding expedition that they fell upon the rear-forlorn of our horse and put it in some disorder; and indeed had like to have engaged our rear-brigade of horse with their whole army – had not the Lord by his Providence put a cloud over the Moon; thereby giving us opportunity to draw off those horse to the rest of our Army.'[1]

The English newspaper *Mercurius Politicus* gave substantially the same account, if giving God somewhat less credit for the English army's escape: 'the enemy drew up a strong party to our rearguard, and might probably have spoyld them if not providentially prevented by the overshaddowing clouds which so eclipsed the moone as thereby a period was put to the enemies' motion.'[2] Although it received little credit, the English field artillery also helped to delay the Scottish vanguard by Monck's having two guns expressly positioned on high ground to help cover the retreat.[3] The English messenger Cadwell put the strength of the Scottish pursuers at 400 horse supported by 400 musketeers, but, typically, Cromwell declared the English losses during the encounter to be trifling, just three or four men from the 'forlorn hope' stationed to cover the retreat of the main body – although clearly it must have been an anxious time for his tired soldiers.

The Scots kept up the pressure, at the very least denying most of their opponents any much needed rest. Around midnight Leslie's cavalry made a noisy attempt to break into the English lines on the south side of Haddington, by charging up to the town's gates and even into its streets. The attack, however, was repulsed after an hour's mêlée, in which Colonel Fairfax's regiment was heavily involved. However short their night's rest, on the following morning – namely that of Sunday 1 September – Cromwell marched his army out of the town 'into an open field on the south side of Haddington and once more offered battle, in order to give [the enemy] way to come to us, if he had so thought fit.'[4] There his bedraggled Puritan soldiers, still confident in their commander and their God, painstakingly cleaned and readied their weapons, publicly said their prayers, sang their psalms and waited. Although the strength of the English army was much reduced and, according to Cromwell, the Scots had just received the addition of three fresh regiments, which, he said, 'did much heighten their confidence, if not presumption and arrogancy',[5] Leslie did not attack.

After about four hours Cromwell gave the signal for his men to move on to Dunbar and after despatching its carriages and guns, the main English army stepped off 'in very tempestuous weather'. If Leslie had really fancied his chances in open battle, Haddington presented an obvious opportunity for him to fight, although it must not be forgotten that the Scottish army had itself suffered grievously, not from Cromwell's actions but from those of the special commission appointed to remove any so-called Malignants (men guilty of supporting Charles I) from it. By the end of August this had cashiered between 3,000 and 4,000 men, for the most part experienced and enthusiastic soldiers, whom one contemporary observer reckoned had been replaced by 'ministers' sons, clerks and such other sanctified creatures, who hardly ever saw or heard of any sword but that of the spirit.'[6] However valuable the addition of three new regiments might be, the rest of the army would still be highly unsettled, or worse. Yet on such an equal field Leslie might still have reasonably expected his fresher and larger army to weigh in his favour, for in such a situation neither army could mount a surprise attack. Weakened as they were, the English were still veteran Ironsides supported by their unmatchable cavalry. Some have attributed Leslie's decision not to attack to the influence of the ministers accompanying the army, who did not favour it – although they would prove far less cautious later[7] – but he might reasonably have been waiting for a better opportunity when, with disease so widespread, Cromwell's numbers would have fallen still further.

Leslie made no further move to impede the English withdrawal from Haddington to Dunbar, although their route was marked by a trail of equipment, including tents, discarded by the sickly and exhausted men. In a preconceived move, the Scots left the coastal road to occupy the commanding feature of Doon Hill about two miles to the south of the port and overlooking its peninsula. While Leslie had rejected the opportunity of fighting at Haddington, he had once again chosen a virtually unassailable position for his army: where Doon Hill faced Dunbar its slope was too

Chapter 7

Delivering Them into Our Hands

Men of prayer, men of war.
(Alfred the Great)

Unlike the tough options facing the Scottish commanders that morning, the courses of action for the English seemed straightforward, namely to strengthen their defence lines and watch events unfold. Although the Scots had already brought some of their cavalry down from Doon Hill to the flatter ground on their side of the Spott or Brox Burn,[1] they could conceivably have been moving them off their exposed positions rather than preparing for a major offensive. In any case, with their 'perspective glasses' focused on Doon Hill, the English commanders could feel reasonably confident the Scots would not make any important moves without their knowledge. Sure enough, somewhat after midday they commenced a major descent and at about 4 p.m. any possible doubts ended when Leslie brought his artillery down, a difficult and protracted operation needing teams of straining horses and ropes to ease the heavy ordnance down the hill's steep and slippery slopes. Once the artillery was down, the rest of the army followed.

The watching Cromwell and his fellow commanders, aware of their reduced strength, were sure to have been impressed by the large numbers of 'Jockies' moving into position before them, especially after being told the opposing army numbered 'six thousand horse and sixteen thousand foot at least', almost double their own strength. The process went on until the early evening but long before all his units were down, Leslie must have realized the tactical shortcomings of placing his cavalry on the flanks, particularly since his left-hand one consisted of a narrow corridor of sloping land fronted by the Spott Burn flowing through a wide gully forty feet deep. As a consequence he moved most of his cavalry from the left across to the more open land on the right to join his other cavalry there, 'causing his right wing of horse to edge down towards the sea',[2] while at the same time he 'shogged' his artillery train and two of his infantry brigades towards the right.

Such repositioning was only to be expected from someone with Leslie's appreciation of ground. It was also a necessary measure for his projected attack towards Broxmouth

House early the next morning, which he planned to make with strong heavy columns 'whose momentum would crumple up the English.'[3] To achieve such weight of offensive and administer a decisive blow he needed to mass his cavalry and artillery within a relatively small area. However, on this occasion if he really believed the English had already shipped off many men together with the heavier of their guns and since he had been pressed into making such an attack by his committee, Leslie might not have positioned all his troops as skilfully as he had in the past and certainly not in anticipation of any aggressive moves by the English. The likely positions taken up by the Scottish army on the evening of 2 September are shown on the map below.

Conversely, the watching English became sure of an impending Scottish strike. As Cromwell himself remarked, 'We could not well imagine but that the enemy intended to attempt upon us or to place themselves in a more exact condition of interposition.'[4] It also appeared to them that such an offensive would not be long delayed for, after

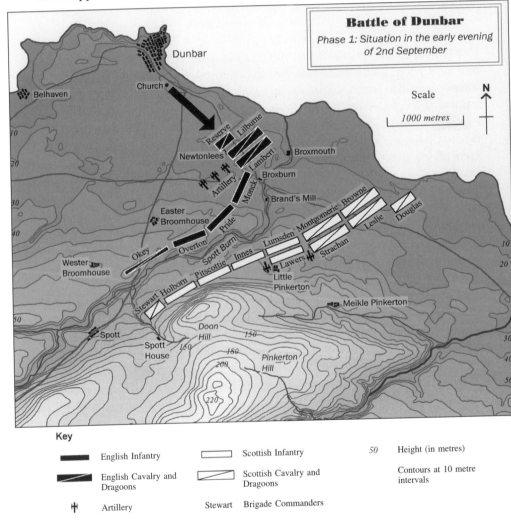

Battle of Dunbar

Phase 1: Situation in the early evening
of 2nd September

Scale

|___ 1000 metres ___|

N

Key

▬▬ English Infantry	▭ Scottish Infantry	*50*	Height (in metres)
▬▬ English Cavalry and Dragoons	▱ Scottish Cavalry and Dragoons		Contours at 10 metre intervals
♯ Artillery	Stewart Brigade Commanders		

moving the bulk of their cavalry onto the open ground to the right of their line, at about 4 p.m. the Scots made a number of attacks on the English outposts. In one of these a cavalry patrol captured a lone building (probably on the site of the present Brand's Mill[5]) guarding one of the crossing places across the burn little more than half a mile from Broxmouth House. The night before, the English had put thirty soldiers and six cavalrymen in it but, when two troops of Scottish lancers attacked, the six English troopers fled and the Scots went on to kill three infantry soldiers and take another three prisoner. After apparently giving promise of quarter, they cut up and drove the rest away.

One of the prisoners was an old soldier with only one good arm, the other being fashioned of wood with an iron hook attached to its end. Notwithstanding, he succeeded in discharging his musket three times against his attackers and was only overpowered after a struggle. He was taken back to David Leslie, who interrogated him, commencing with the question, 'How will you fight when you have shipped half your men and all your great guns?' The veteran's rejoinder came in the form of a counter-question: what did he think they came there for? They came for nothing else [but to fight]. 'Sir if you please to draw down with your army you will find both men and great guns also.'[6] At this one of Leslie's staff asked the Ironside how dared he answer the general so saucily, receiving the stout reply he had only made answer to the question demanded of him.

There have been different interpretations about these questions of Leslie's here; Samuel Gardiner considered they revealed his firm belief that Cromwell had actually shipped his guns along with very many men and that he was in fact seeking confirmation from the soldier,[7] while W S Douglas believed they were designed to make the soldier blurt out the information he sought.[8] But with such an astute old soldier, Leslie himself appeared in danger of suffering a double bluff. Whatever his conclusions, he was reported to have told his soldiers that by seven o'clock the next morning they would 'have the English army dead or alive',[9] and he finally called for a trumpeter to signal the return of the old soldier to the English lines. There Cromwell was informed of the dialogue and, furthermore, the old warrior claimed that twenty shillings had been taken from him during the action, at which Cromwell recompensed him with two pieces (forty shillings) from his own purse.

The incident showed both commanders in a humane light, although Leslie should already have taken care to place an observer in Dunbar to give him accurate news on whether the English had in fact shipped out their great guns, while Cromwell's gift of forty shillings to the canny old soldier suggested he had a more subtle sense of humour than many of his contemporaries imagined. The soldier's demeanour might also have confirmed Cromwell's belief that, whatever their predicament and however highly tried such soldiers might be, men of that stamp were still capable of achieving remarkable things under his direction.

Cromwell was soon to put them to the test, for, whatever his sense of humour, no one could ever doubt his aggressive intentions. Apparently, after watching the lengthy manoeuvrings of the large Scottish army he turned to Lambert standing beside him and observed that the position of the Scots army appeared 'to give us an opportunity and advantage'. During this exchange Carlyle has Cromwell saying, 'Here is the enemy's right wing coming out to the open space, free to be attacked on any side; and now the main battle hampered in narrow sloping ground between Doon Hill and the Brook, has no room to manoeuvre or assist: beat this right wing where it now stands; take it in flank and front with an overpowering force – it is driven upon its own main battle, the whole Army is beaten.'[10]

Whether these were Cromwell's actual words or this is an instance of Carlyle's wisdom after the event, they caught the essential thinking of a man whose aim was to destroy his enemy and who sensed that here was an utterly unexpected, but no less genuine, opportunity to do so. Captain Hodgson reputedly heard him exclaim, 'God is delivering them into our hands, they are coming down to us',[11] and Professor Gardiner concluded later that Cromwell's confidence in being able to achieve it came from his consciousness 'that in his army he possessed an instrument of war unequalled in its day',[12] while the Scots were fatally overconfident. This has not stopped one writer from continuing to believe that Cromwell never intended to destroy the Scottish army but rather aimed to brush it aside in order to 'force open the Berwick road and escape southwards'.[13] Certainly the odds against the English on this occasion were awesome, even for Cromwell and his Puritan Ironsides, who were far from ordinary soldiers. Characteristically, while Cromwell paid credit to God for his inspiration to mount such an attack, in practice he did not neglect to consult Lambert about its feasibility. Lambert, a brilliant, aggressive soldier in his own right – and markedly less eager to ascribe any such inspiration to his God – replied that he had thought to say the same thing to his leader. Captain Hodgson, writing some twenty years later, went further still, having Lambert take the initiative himself. Following his discussion with Lambert, Cromwell went on to consult Monck, the army's acknowledged tactician, about whether he too could see an opportunity to attack. Monck quickly acknowledged he could, and urged Cromwell to do so before the Scots could mount theirs. Having thus made up their minds, the three decided to ride into Dunbar in search of food.

With a force so reduced in number and ravaged by illness, the daring of the decision to strike at an army almost twice their strength needs no emphasis. It went against all the normal canons of war, which required attackers to possess superior numbers, and its whole success depended upon the Scots not being able to deploy a considerable number of their men. Most important, to have any chance of winning it required a major reordering during the night under the very noses of their opponents – and if this were not enough – its intended *pièce de résistance* relied upon a flanking march past standing enemy formations. In no other battle since 1644 had a commander knowingly accepted such adverse odds for what Cromwell acknowledged would be his 'masterpiece or his Misfortune', nor had such a full tactical plan been made beforehand. In the past, once the two sides were drawn up and the orders given to attack, the outcome had largely depended upon the success of individual formations: at Marston Moor, upon the recovery and subsequent inspired conduct of the

Parliamentary cavalry; at Edgehill upon the superlative performance of Prince Rupert's cavalry, and at Naseby upon the skilled use by Fairfax and Cromwell of their larger numbers of horse.

While Cromwell's plan at Dunbar was not particularly complicated, its preparations certainly were, and so bold were they that success relied on hair-trigger co-ordination. With such adverse force balances there was virtually no margin for error, especially if the Scots were to respond in the gallant and skilful manner they had already shown on so many occasions during the previous five weeks. Yet whoever first saw the opportunity, and however high the risks, Cromwell, as commander in chief, could be confident of enjoying singular support from Lambert and Monck in his attempts to carry it out. Whatever Leslie's numerical advantages, he did not have such supporting commanders.

While Cromwell, Lambert and Monck were eating (and considering their battle plans) instructions were sent out for the necessary council of war. After the time so recently spent perfecting the army's defensive positions, notice of a fresh council of war was bound to raise a host of rumours. With such a leader, any new proposals seemed likely to involve serious, if not desperate, fighting, and in view of the army's present condition, this prospect was probably not universally popular. According to Captain Hodgson, the council took place at nine o'clock that night, although it almost certainly started earlier, and Cromwell left the task of advocating the hazardous offensive to the widely popular and charismatic Jack Lambert. When the council opened, many of the army's colonels were of the opinion that after their recent five weeks of underachievement, and with the army's numbers fallen so low (and continuing to fall) they should accept – for this campaign at least – that they were beaten. Some proposed shipping the infantry out while the cavalry broke through at the extremity of the Scottish lines to make its best way overland to England.

Such suggestions were very likely to have aroused Cromwell's temper and caused him to raise his considerable voice, but Lambert did not allow himself to be so moved, coolly demolishing the colonels' proposals on account of their riskiness! He then gave a confident and detailed explanation (giving them the chance to check the ground for themselves) about how the present position of the Scots

> gave us reasons and great encouragement to fight. Firstly we had great experience of the goodness of God to us while we kept close together; if we parted we lost all. Secondly there was no time to ship the foot, for the day would be upon us. Thirdly we had great advantages of them in their drawing up; if we beat their right wing, we hazarded their whole army, for they could be all in confusion, in regard they had not great ground to traverse their regiments betwixt the mountains and the clough. Fourthly they had left intervals in their bodies upon the brink of the hill and the enemy could not wheel about nor oppose [our horse and foot] but must put themselves in disorder. Lastly our guns might have fair play at their left wing while we were fighting the right.[14]

With Lambert making it clear that Cromwell intended to attack, strongly supported here by himself and Monck, and that they proposed to compensate for the imbalance in numbers by unhinging the Scottish formations, the council agreed to their plan. As a dubious reward, Cromwell gave his eloquent spokesman the additional responsibility of both reordering the army and then conducting the initial offensive the next morning. Thomas Gumble, Monck's biographer, wrongly put Monck instead of Lambert in charge of the attack, although Monck undoubtedly made an important contribution by personally leading four of the army's infantry regiments.

During the hours of darkness Lambert had to reposition the army and make it ready for an attack due to begin at about 4 o'clock the next morning. This involved moving virtually all the English units out of their appointed positions and sending some closer to the two chief crossing points over the burn, namely at the main road and at Brand's Mill, thus giving Lambert and Monck the manpower for their projected attacks on the infantry and cavalry formations occupying the Scottish right centre, while Colonel Thomas Pride's brigade and Cromwell's own reserve would be brought leftward, closer to the coast, in order to deliver the second and hopefully decisive blows. To fill the positions vacated in the English battle lines, four companies of Colonel John Okey's dragoons would be despatched to throw out a lengthy but thin covering line along the banks of the Spott Burn opposite its wide ravine. Finally, Lambert, assisted by Colonel Richard Deane, the artillery expert brought from London, had to concentrate the artillery train and bring it forward into a protruding bend of the burn, where it would be able to play upon both flanks of the Scottish units, particularly those positioned in the pocket where the burn ran through its ravine. This was undoubtedly the single most difficult manoeuvre of the whole night.

No earlier British battle had required such extensive reordering at night and in such proximity to the enemy. The nearest comparison is probably Robert Bruce's management of his army at Bannockburn when, as the sky began to lighten, he moved his spearmen down an escarpment and across open ground before they formed their start line and began hemming a vastly superior English army into a deadly pocket. Such extensive reordering as Lambert's could never have been accomplished by an inexperienced army and without highly competent commanders, to colonel level or below. Even so, Lambert was in the saddle all night shepherding tired and half-blind men across uneven and soaked ground into their battle stations. No one in the English army had any rest that night, although once in position some of the old soldiers would have doubtless cat-napped where they stood, but however many stumblings, contrary orders and misunderstandings that must have occurred in the darkness, all would have understood the need to mask their movements as best they could from the nearby Scottish soldiers.

For many of the English, the consciousness of the far larger numbers of Scots and the forthcoming battle helped to provoke much enthusiastic and characteristic Puritan praying – fervently and out loud. Towards morning, Captain Hodgson and his men from Lambert's own regiment were ordered to march down to Broxmouth House where, not for the first time in that campaign, they stripped down for action, discarding their tents and baggage. Having done so, towards the head of the horse they heard a young cornet pouring out his prayers. Hodgson could not resist riding over, the better to hear the young supplicant and, as he expressed it, 'he was exceedingly carried on in the duty'. It was a mark of the religious core in the Puritan army that the young man's fervour genuinely impressed and heartened the veteran Hodgson, who felt 'There was so much of God in it as I was satisfied deliverance was at hand.'[15] So much so, that he immediately returned to his command and encouraged his own 'poor weak soldiers to pray also'. With such an arduous task before them, many other sectaries would have opened dialogues with their Lord that night, although the less devout Lambert, with the most responsible task of all, spent virtually all his energy on seeing the army took up its battle positions.

It was otherwise with his leader, Cromwell, who, although never happier than when preparing for battle, would have had few illusions about the risks on this occasion. He therefore consciously moved round his army, preceded by a torchbearer and riding a stocky Scottish pony, stopping on endless occasions to talk with his troops, his own depth of concern apparent from the way he was biting his lip. Close to dawn, when all Lambert's efforts were obviously taking shape, Cromwell became more optimistic, appearing to be in a near-religious ecstasy, and 'carried on as with a divine impulse'.[16]

For his Ironsides, whatever their previous battle experiences, those hours of darkness on 2–3 September must have been unforgettable. During that wild night nature itself seemed enraged, the howling wind and periodic gusts of rain being accompanied by the deeper and more rhythmic boom of waves crashing against the nearby cliffs. For most of it, the Stygian darkness was only briefly relieved by the moon's fitful appearances from behind massed clouds. Inevitably, there were the sights and sounds of the English soldiers as they criss-crossed bearing flickering torches, and pinpricks of light danced from the musketeers' fuses; while the snorts of horses together with the jingling of their tackle and the crunch of wagon wheels, interspersed with urgent shouts from gun crews wrestling with their ungainly charges, overbore the rhythmic tramping of the soldiers. Most dramatic of all, about an hour before dawn when most soldiers were in position and standing outwardly relaxed and ready, the clouds parted and everything was illuminated by a large harvest moon.

* * * *

The Scottish army was subject to the same weather conditions, of course, although their pattern of activity was markedly different from that of the English. During a day largely spent by the English in checking their defensive positions, the Scots had been heavily engaged in the physically demanding task of bringing their whole army, together with its equipment, down the steep sides of Doon Hill and taking up new positions on the valley floor. No sooner had they settled themselves in orthodox formations, with their infantry units flanked by cavalry, than Leslie had given orders

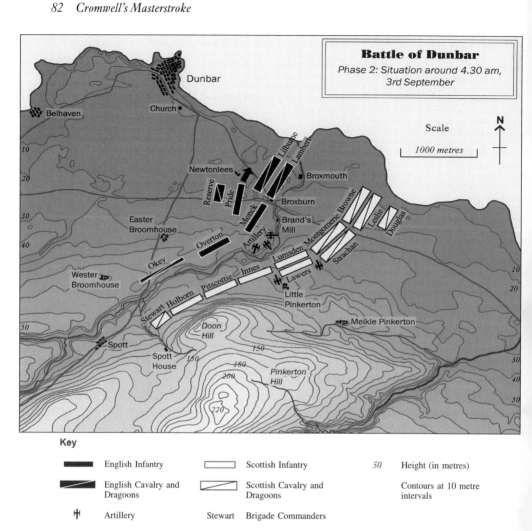

Battle of Dunbar

Phase 2: Situation around 4.30 am, 3rd September

Key

▬▬ English Infantry	▭ Scottish Infantry	*50* Height (in metres)
▨▨ English Cavalry and Dragoons	▨ Scottish Cavalry and Dragoons	Contours at 10 metre intervals
⊞ Artillery	Stewart Brigade Commanders	

to move much of the cavalry from the far left to the more open area on the right, from where they could better attack Broxmouth House the next morning.

Like so much else in this Scottish conduct, nothing is known about their second council of war, although with the complexity of their move down Doon Hill and the projected attacks, it would have been obligatory to hold one. As well as this lack of knowledge there are only the sparsest details about the tactical responsibilities shouldered by the infantry brigade commanders, Lumsden, Holborn, Pitscottie, Campbell of Lawers and Innes, although, as major general of foot, Holborn appears to have been accountable for keeping the army alert during that night. And although General Robert Montgomerie, Leslie's valued friend, was responsible for commanding the first line of Scottish cavalry, the part he must have played in planning the offensive operations remains unrecorded. In practice, Leslie could well have left much of the detailed planning for the assault, together with the actual conduct of operations, to any or all of these.

rles II (artist unknown).
By courtesy of the Scottish National Portrait Gallery.

1st Marquis of Argyll (attributed to David Scougall).
By courtesy of the Scottish National Portrait Gallery.

id Leslie (by 11th Earl of Buchan).
a private Scottish collection, by arrangement with the ish National Portrait Gallery.

Alexander Leslie, Earl of Leven (attributed to George Jamesone).
By courtesy of the Scottish National Portrait Gallery.

Oliver Cromwell (after Samuel Cooper).
By courtesy of the National Portrait Gallery, London.

General Sir John Lambert (after Robert Walker).
By courtesy of the National Portrait Gallery, London.

Fitz-Payne Fisher's map of Dunbar. The engraving was intended to illustrate the Englis
army's victory at Dunbar. In fact its positioning of the two armies gives an inaccurate
representation of what actually occurred. *By courtesy of the Ashmolean Museum, Oxfo*

Scottish pikemen at the time of Dunbar.

English musketeers with their matches clearly visible.

A saker cannon in 1650.

Digital images: Paul Vickers.

Belhaven   Dunbar harbour   Dunbar church   New

Easter Broomhouse   Spott Burn

Panorama of Dunbar battle area from Doon Hill.

The Spott Burn at Brand's Mill.

Broxburn   Broxmouth

Brand's Mill

Photographs: Paul Vickers.

The ravine, showing its high crumbly banks and the Spott Burn running through marshy ground.

The route traversed by Cromwell when making his flank attack.   *Photographs: Paul Vicker*

Present view of Dunbar from the shore, showing the parish church and Doon Hill over looking the town.

The old parish church at Dunbar.

By courtesy of the Dunbar and District History Society.

Spott church.

Photograph: Barbara Reese.

Carlyle might, of course, have been right in thinking that by now Leslie had come to believe that Cromwell was lost[17] and had accordingly consciously relaxed his normal stern discipline. Such an assumption against Cromwell and his veteran army would, of course, have been highly dangerous, but no one – Kirkmen, Leven, Montgomerie nor Leslie himself – could have anticipated the English launching an all-out assault upon them. Nonetheless, the unwillingness on the part of the Scottish leaders to consider the full range of options open to their opponents – the almost unthinkable as well as the obvious – led them to act in a purblind way. Absorbed by the problems attending their forthcoming attacks, they positioned the horse quite close to the sea, thereby extending their battle lines to the obvious benefit of any would-be attacker. Drawn up in formations ready for the next morning's attack, most of their soldiers slept on the ground as best they could during the course of that 'drakie nycht full of wind and weit'.

Yet, however bad the weather, with even a half-efficient system of sentries they must have been aware of some repositioning by the English. Sure enough, during the earlier part of the night such movements caused the Scots to raise the alarm on two occasions but, with no further outcome from them, the soldiers resumed their broken rest. Some of the infantry lying in the fields built considerable shelters from corn stooks and slept within them, while the cavalry went foraging and unsaddled not just their first but many of their second line horses too. Arguably the most irresponsible act during that stormy and fateful night came when General Holborn conducted an inspection of the forward companies (the only senior Scottish commander recorded as doing so) and agreed that in such adverse conditions all but two musketeers per company could extinguish the matches for their muskets.

Such instances of laxness by forward troops with the enemy but a stone's throw away need no emphasizing, but, worse still, many of the officers, middle-rank as well as the most senior, apparently left the battle lines altogether to seek shelter at Spott Farm in East Barns or at Meikle and Easter Pinkerton lying behind Doon Hill. Although it was undoubtedly easier to keep discipline among men who were on the move like the English, and while weather conditions during most of the night were dire, discipline in the Scottish army was undoubtedly slack, making it far more difficult to respond quickly and effectively to an 'impossible' attack by the English the next day.

Across the burn Lambert had, of course, been readying his Puritan troopers for that very action, but at the appointed time for the assault, and with Cromwell fretting on the start line, there was no sign of him. Reports that he was with the artillery, whose crews had experienced frightful difficulties manhandling their pieces into position, were unlikely to have satisfied Cromwell, quite justifiably, for with the sky lightening all the English exertions could yet be wasted. If the Scots were to realize the nature and extent of such preparations they could even now bring superior numbers to counter them.

Chapter 8

Face to Face

The essential agony of the battle.
(Thomas Carlyle)

Cromwell's concern was well founded: if his plans for an all-out attack were to misfire and he failed to detach his shattered forces and move them back into Dunbar, he would have to surrender. In addition, although the reordering of his army was virtually complete, a serious snag had arisen which patently did not improve his hopes for success when the units despatched by Lambert about forty-five minutes before to occupy the start line for the cavalry's attack had clashed with a party of Scottish horse. Although Cromwell did not know it, the Scottish horsemen had themselves been committed to clearing a route for a subsequent attack on Broxmouth House, with the further understanding that, in the event of the English defenders proving slack, they could press on with their own attack upon the house.

The resultant skirmish was described by the English messenger Cadwell as lasting 'for an hour and [it] was very hot, the great guns playing on both sides very hot on each other's main body'.[1] In spite of the messenger's account, it is improbable that many, if any, of the guns opened up on each other at this stage but, in any case, the sounds of musket fire coming from the vicinity of the ford would probably have led Cromwell to believe that the Scots were also in full readiness and any chance of him springing a surprise had much diminished, if not disappeared. The English great guns were unlikely to have been used this early for, although Lambert and Deane had positioned them on a bend of the Brox Burn close to Brand's Mill, from where they could enfilade both flanks of the Scottish positions, the light was still decidedly poor. In turn, the lighter Scottish ordnance that had been placed level with their forward cavalry lines to support the projected crossings of the burn were probably taken unawares. They were unlikely to have been ready for immediate action, with many of their vents too damp to receive the priming powder. And with some of the Scottish horse moving across their front they were not well positioned to cannonade any English units moving out from the vicinity of Broxmouth House.

Whatever the extent of the firefight, Cromwell, helmeted and gauntleted, sitting astride a full-size cavalry horse, chafed furiously at the delay, but moments later Lambert galloped up with the welcome news that the English forward units had succeeded in securing the crossing points. He was also able to give Cromwell instances of continuing Scottish unpreparedness – for example, some of the cavalry had actually been caught in their tents. On their left flank, young Bannatyne of Corhouse, son to the Lieutenant Colonel of Colonel Stewart's regiment of horse, had only 'narrowly escaped being knocked on the head or made prisoner, for his father's tent was cut down above him before he could get to horse.'[2]

It was now after 5 a.m., with sunrise at 5.33,[3] when Lambert's cavalry brigade finally splashed across the ford at the main road and moved towards the Scottish cavalry. The brigade included his own regiment, accompanied by those of Fleetwood and Whalley. With the masses of Scottish cavalry so close, an experienced commander like Lambert would have been fully aware of his force's vulnerability, either while crossing, or immediately on the far side. In fact, they were unchallenged, and once across he brought his troopers into close formation before taking them at a steady gallop up the gentle clover-covered slopes towards the dense lines of Scottish cavalry occupying the open ground some 400 yards away. From here the Scots were well placed to launch their own attacks towards Broxmouth House; even so they appeared far from ready to meet him. In accordance with Cromwell's master plan Lambert directed his men towards the Scots' foremost ranks commanded by General Robert Montgomerie. If Lambert could knock out the squadrons on the Scottish right wing, he could (with support from Lilburne's brigade following close behind) then swing round and take their others in the flank or even the rear. At the least the attack would deny the Scottish cavalry the opportunity to move across and meet the English infantry when it set off on its intended attack, which in normal circumstances they could confidently expect to ride down.

While their riders might be tired, the English had taken care to keep their first-choice mounts in good condition, helped here by the ample quantities of good grass presently available after so much rain. Riding in compact formation, they trotted forward until their heavy horses closed right up with their adversaries before discharging their pistols or carbines at point-blank range. In the event, they struck at opponents experiencing serious difficulties of control; General Montgomerie was still absent and many other officers and troopers had yet to take up their places in the forward lines when the English volley started emptying saddles. The lighter Scottish cavalry were particularly vulnerable since most of their riders were equipped with lances together with daggers (skean dhus for the Highlanders and dirks for the others) rather than firearms. In the right circumstances such lances, with their fearsome points and sideward-facing spikes resembling small Lochaber axes, could be used to telling effect, and the Scottish horsemen had already excelled themselves during the English withdrawal from Musselburgh a few days before.

However, on the morning of 3 September they were themselves under attack and their problems were compounded by the unwelcome and unexpected appearance of

Battle of Dunbar
Phase 3: Situation around 5.30 am,
3rd September

Scale
1000 metres

N

Key

▬▬ English Infantry	▭ Scottish Infantry	*50*	Height (in metres)
▬ English Cavalry and Dragoons	◰ Scottish Cavalry and Dragoons		Contours at 10 metre intervals
╫ Artillery	Stewart Brigade Commanders		

some cannonballs from the assembled English guns skidding along the grass among their rearward ranks.

Such an unexpected assault from better armed, if smaller numbers, of opposing cavalry supported by artillery massed at the curve of the burn, might well have created some sense of panic among soldiers from a lesser fighting tradition. But this was not the conduct expected from Scottish soldiers, who earlier, under the leadership of William Wallace at Falkirk and James IV at Flodden, had fought on long after all hopes of victory had been lost, and at Dunbar most of them stood firm despite the severe dislocation caused by successive 'purgings' of experienced soldiers (the last of which had been carried out the very night before the battle),[4] their considerable casualties and the absence of many of their commanders.

While the Scottish horse were receiving the hammer blows of Lambert's heavy cavalry, the signal was given for George Monck and his infantry brigade to begin their own attack. With the prospect of a fight his soldiers had shaken off their fatigue and in their already damp clothing they made little of splashing through the ford at Brand's Mill, before making their best way up the burn's steep bank on the far side. The attack by the English cavalry had already alerted the Scottish army to other likely assaults and Monck had no need to conceal his movements. Once across, his brigade formed up with its musketeers in front and the pikemen standing close behind, keeping their weapons in the vertical position. Upon Monck's command it set off steadily to cover the 300 or so yards of gently sloping pasture between them and Sir James Lumsden's large Scottish brigade. To give themselves heart the English soldiers roared out their battle cry 'The Lord of Hosts!', bringing the inevitable response from those awaiting them of 'The Covenant!' A good proportion of the English wore red jackets, in contrast to the dun ones of their opponents, and that morning there was a further and deliberate distinction between the two sides, with the Roundheads being forbidden from wearing any white pieces of dress. On their move forward, like the cavalry a little earlier, the English foot soldiers became aware of considerable activity in the Scottish lines, marked with a flurry of trumpet calls and men still hastening to occupy their places in the front ranks. Equally important, the forward Ironsides could see lighted matches being passed among the Scots musketeers. After about 200 yards Monck halted for his men to fire a concerted volley, which at such short range, despite the inaccuracy of their weapons, found many victims. The opposing lines shivered, gaps appeared and screams of pain were heard as heavy musket balls thudded against bone and sinew. The musketeers then found themselves vulnerable to the Scots' counter-fire while performing the detailed series of actions necessary for reloading, but this proved less heavy than might have been expected and with their weapons recharged, the English set off again. After firing a second volley at hardly more than fifty yards, the musketeers ran to the flanks, cartwheeling their weapons in order to use their butts as clubs. It was now the turn of the English pikemen who, at the appropriate drum roll, lowered their long spears to the horizontal and stepped forward to counter the outstretched spears on the Scottish side, seeking to exploit the gaps already created in their opponents' ranks.

Monck's veterans undoubtedly enjoyed the best of things early on, but if the Scots could preserve their cohesion their larger numbers would soon be bound to come into play. Cromwell had selected Lumsden's brigade for attack because by keeping it fully pinned down, the Scottish units to its left would be stopped from moving across and entering the battle. As luck had it, although the brigade was far larger than Monck's, it was much the rawest unit in the Scottish army, being made up of Highland levies that had reached Haddington only three days before. This – like the Scottish cavalry in the opening encounters – also suffered from an absence of officers, including its commanding officer, a loss all the more serious with an inexperienced unit. To add to its problems, while the English soldiers jabbed with their pikes and swung their muskets against the foremost ranks, with the improving light, the English guns began to play upon this flank as well, opening up bloody corridors in the brigade's rearward lines, and firing deep into the pocket manned by the Scottish infantry between the base of Doon Hill and the ravine carrying the Spott Burn. Similar carnage against massed formations had resulted at the earlier Battle of Newbury, where a Captain John Gwyn observed 'a whole file of men, six deep, with their heads struck off with one cannon shot'.[5] In spite of such initial successes, the physical effort needed to wield their long and unwieldy pikes in such a close-quarter mêlée promised to tire Monck's soldiers, who were already in poor physical condition, more quickly than their more numerous opponents. In any case an army which up to now had consistently outflanked and harried the English until their numbers were diminished and exhausted, could be expected to retaliate more positively than by mere endurance.

Despite the Scots' initial setbacks the fruits of this were soon evident, in the first instance on the open ground closer to the sea where Lambert and his cavalry were attacking. Following his initial blows upon Montgomerie's first-line squadron in which English small arms had brought down many riders, both sides came close enough to swing at each other with their swords; the English then deliberately drew back slightly (as Cromwell had taught them) to regain their formation and ready their horses for a second telling strike. Before they could do so, Colonel Archibald Strachan, who (whatever his problems of allegiance later) had already proved himself a first-rate cavalry commander, reacted swiftly. Leading forward his second-line troopers, whom he had trained thoroughly in the use of their lances, he forced Lambert's brigade to give some ground, causing the heavier but now outnumbered English cavalry to find themselves in considerable danger.

As for the infantry, although George Monck might have inflicted serious blows on Lumsden's brigade and despite Lumsden himself becoming its most notable casualty, the two sides were now closed up and with likely help from the adjacent Campbell of Lawers's brigade the sheer weight of Scottish numbers was bound to have an effect. Accordingly, after halting Monck's brigade, they forced it by push of pike to give ground until, despite the best English efforts, they were driven backwards down the rough slope to their original position. Here Monck probably called for reinforcements from Overton's brigade guarding the artillery close by, but whether these reached him or not, both sides now stood in apparent impasse, with neither yet prepared to resume what promised to be a sanguinary encounter. Yet so intent were Lumsden's brigade on their very survival, they had not been able to release any other formations confined in the pocket between the base of Doon Hill and the burn, who in any case were being heavily scourged by the English guns.

With the apparent success of the Scottish responses so far, a contemporary observer might have reasonably expected the larger side eventually to win the day. What he could not have anticipated at this point were the contrasting roles to be played by the respective commanders at Dunbar, with those on the English side well aware of, and adhering to, Cromwell's blueprint, while Leslie had radically to change his. Since the afternoon of the previous day, when he had been preparing to attack, followed by a tempestuous night which had limited his early offensive measures to a single foray, Leslie could have been forgiven for thinking the English would have been similarly affected[6] in what he so recently believed were attempts to strengthen their defences.

In any case, in view of the widely reported poor physical state of the English troops and their far smaller numbers, Leslie and his fellow commanders had genuine reasons to feel confident and to believe their opponents were not only trapped but ready for the taking. Such thinking helps to explain their neglect to put out scouts and monitor the English activities. As the contemporary observer Nicoll expressed it, 'Our Scottis army wer' careless and secure expecting no assault.'[7]

Whatever the reasons, it was not until about 4.30 a.m. on the morning of 3 September, after Leslie's initial scouting force had been despatched, that the fierceness of the fire coming from the point where the burn crossed the main road alerted him (like Cromwell) to a possible new situation. Unfortunately, because of the lack of Scottish accounts of the battle, nothing is known about the pattern of Leslie's activities or of his responses at this time. That he was on the battlefield from the time the first shot was fired seems indisputable, for the subsequent inquiry into the outcome of the battle brought no condemnation of Leslie's personal conduct there. In spite of strong local beliefs that Leslie actually spent the night to the rear of the Scottish positions in the comfort of Spott House, it is far more likely that while he might well have taken dinner there he would have directed operations from the large tent traditionally used by Scottish commanders in chief, pitched directly behind his massed cavalry squadrons.

At the inquiry Leslie blamed his officers for being negligent and lazy; it is inconceivable that he had sheltered in Spott House or in one of the neighbouring small settlements of Meikle or Little Pinkerton. What Leslie undoubtedly took responsibility for was his positioning of the army. Two days after the battle he wrote, 'I know I get my own share of the salt by many for drawing them so near the enemy, and must suffer in this as in many times formerly; though I take God to witness we might as easily have beaten them as we did James Graham at Philiphaugh if the officers had stayed by their own troops and regiments.'[8] The comparison between Montrose's few weak formations and the still formidable English army seems highly strained, but from his statement soon after the battle it is plain that Leslie almost certainly placed his formations facing the burn and ready to move down the slopes leading to it, and not looking northward as the poet, ex-Royalist and soldier of fortune, Fitz-Payne Fisher, indicated in his later, somewhat fanciful, illustration of the battlefield.[9]

Whatever positions Leslie had selected for his troops on the evening of 2 September, following the initial exchange of musketry fire the following morning his first problem, as for any commander before or since, was to discover exactly what was going on so that he could react accordingly. When the firing in the vicinity of the burn was followed up by major and wholly unexpected attacks by the English, he had to establish how heavy they were, against whom they were directed and what they might prefigure. Shortly before dawn on that stormy morning such answers were not easily forthcoming; periodic heavy showers, low-lying mist and the smoke from musket fire would have restricted visibility along the valley and across the low ground to the right of the main road. In such circumstances he would have needed to send outriders across the battlefield to discover the true picture and bring him back the details. In any event, Leslie's responses were bound to have been hampered by the late arrival on the field of so many of his key officers. Whatever his particular difficulties of command that morning, the manner of the English attacks was also beyond Leslie's battlefield experience: he had been the attacker at Marston Moor, as later when hunting Montrose, and although his present campaign against Cromwell had initially been one of manoeuvre and avoidance, latterly Leslie had again taken up the pursuit.

Another unanswered question concerning the Scottish forces that morning was, what plans, if any, did Leslie have in mind for his artillery and how might he have adapted them to help meet Cromwell's own attacks? While some of the lighter Scottish guns were almost certainly located alongside their right-hand cavalry and infantry brigades, this was not the case with the main artillery train that Leslie had brought down Doon Hill with so much difficulty. According to the English messenger, Cadwell, the Scottish guns were in action early in the day, and if so it would have been those positioned close to the front of their troops. There are no references to the bulk of the Scottish artillery, which played no significant part in impeding the English movements, unlike the major role played by the massed English artillery, particularly against the left-hand Scottish forces.

Once again Cromwell seemed to reap the benefits of his detailed planning the night before when the English artillery was given a pivotal role. In contrast, it is probable the Scots' offensive plans were drawn up at a somewhat earlier stage, and because of their high confidence in the likely result they may not have included detailed plans for the part to be played by their artillery. In any event, with Leslie's projected attacks on the right involving massed brigades, there would be no similar opportunity to provide enfilading fire. The battlefield on the Scottish left was too shallow for guns to be positioned in this way and the trees and walls on the Broxmouth estate would have limited the effectiveness of mounting a supporting barrage from the right flank. With such difficulties apparent during the planning stages it is probable that the Scottish heavy guns were not given major responsibilities.

The majority of the Scottish artillery were, therefore, probably drawn up some-where close to Leslie's command tent behind his cavalry formations, ready to be deployed where he chose. However, after the surprise English attacks the fluid nature of the subsequent cavalry engagements offered little scope for them to be used and throughout the battle Lumsden's brigade screened Monck's English troops from direct gunfire. Further use of the Scottish artillery appeared to depend upon Leslie's ability to anticipate the nature of Cromwell's follow-up attacks and, if he guessed right, whether there would be enough time for it to help intercept them.

In contrast Cromwell, the vastly more experienced commander, knew exactly what operations his army had mounted so far with both his troops and his ordnance and how he could best use the balance of his troops to exploit them. Equally important, he had ensured that his commanders were fully briefed about his bold designs so that they and their veteran soldiers could be relied upon to carry them out. After spending all night reorganizing the army for the attack, Lambert, with wounds barely healed from the preliminary campaigning, still had sufficient energy and enthusiasm to lead his cavalry brigade in a skilfully directed assault against Leslie's close-packed horse, and with Monck at the head of the infantry attack Cromwell could be sure his troops would retain their cohesion, however fearsome the Scottish response.

In the face of Cromwell's twin attacks Leslie and his commanders had little option but to react as best they could, although, whatever his problems in following the progress of the battle, Leslie was likely to have remained confident: the English attacks so far appeared to have been countered and his numbers remained superior.

In reality, the tide was already moving strongly in the direction of the English. Cromwell had deployed just two brigades, but his others were about to move up in support and he still possessed a powerful reserve. Unlike the Scottish army, many of whose formations were badly positioned, he could use the balance of his forces to restore and extend the impetus of his attacks. In fact, the second English cavalry brigade under Colonel Robert Lilburne, following close behind Lambert's, was about to give it assistance, while the second of Cromwell's three infantry brigades, primarily responsible for guarding the massed English guns, was in a position to provide Monck with additional support. As for Colonel John Okey's dragoons, four of his six companies were actively employed in maintaining a defensive screen, albeit a thin one, along the Dunbar bank of the burn. Despite the relative smallness of his army, Cromwell's fourth infantry brigade under Colonel Thomas Pride, together with his own powerful cavalry regiment and the remaining two companies of dragoons, were able to move into position to make a telling contribution.

Things were strikingly different for the Scottish army. On the left flank three complete infantry brigades, under General Colin Pitscottie, General James Holborn and Colonel John Innes, together with the cavalry brigade of Colonel William Stewart at the far left of the line, remained confined in the relatively narrow corridor of land between Doon Hill and the broad ravine of the Spott Burn. In all, some 9,000 Scottish soldiers – equivalent to 75 per cent of the total English strength – could not be brought into action quickly. This left about 12,000 men, of whom 4,500 were cavalry, to face the 7,500 English soldiers already committed, not counting Cromwell's powerful reserve. The gross disparity between the two armies when they approached Dunbar no longer applied: and man for man the English were the more experienced and better-trained soldiers, although if Leslie could bring just half his soldiers out of their confined position the attacking English would once more be heavily outnumbered. Apart from these units in the pocket, Leslie had greater numbers of horse, where the elements of five brigades with widely differing parade strengths faced Lambert's single brigade presently being joined by Lilburne's. Although Lambert had already dealt a heavy blow against Montgomerie's first-line formations, and each of the two English brigades, mounted on their heavy cavalry horses and bearing small arms, had greater hitting power than their Scottish equivalents, if the more numerous Scottish squadrons could unite to repulse them and then turn against Monck's (and Overton's) infantry, the pattern of the battle would swiftly change. This, however, required complex movements, ones made more difficult still when under attack.

Whatever his tactical ability, Cromwell's chances of success were dependent to a great extent on the fighting skills of Lambert and his veteran troopers, closely supported here by Lilburne. After Lilburne's brigade joined Lambert, they immediately engaged the Scottish cavalry in a number of separate actions across the open ground stretching from Broxmouth House to White Sands in the east. By moving the fighting southward away from the vicinity of Broxmouth House and preventing the Scottish cavalry from intervening elsewhere, they offered Cromwell the opportunity for his further bold and potentially decisive move. This began when Cromwell took Thomas Pride's infantry brigade, together with his own cavalry regiment commanded by Captain Packer, to the far side of Broxmouth House, from where they could cross the Brox Burn with relative ease. Some indication of Cromwell's move can be gained from Fitz-Payne Fisher's engraving of the battle,[10] although a more reliable and accurate reference to it came from the faithful Captain

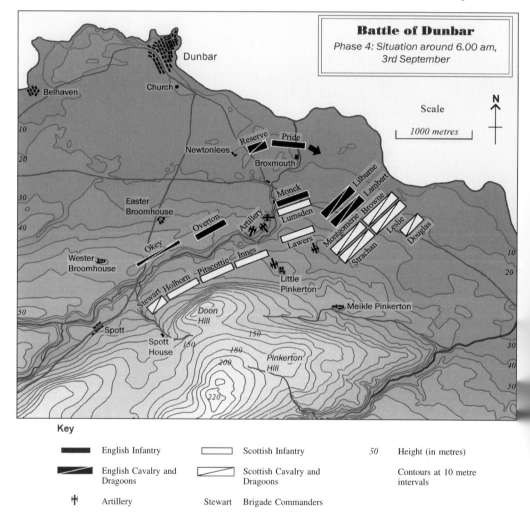

Battle of Dunbar

Phase 4: Situation around 6.00 am, 3rd September

Key

▬▬	English Infantry	☐	Scottish Infantry	*50* Height (in metres)
▬▬	English Cavalry and Dragoons	⬛	Scottish Cavalry and Dragoons	Contours at 10 metre intervals
♯	Artillery	Stewart	Brigade Commanders	

Hodgson: 'At last the Major General came and ordered Packer, major to the General's regiment, Gough's and our two foot regiments to march about Broxmouth House towards the sea and so to fall upon the enemy's flank.'[11]

With the need for speed it is very likely that Cromwell crossed the burn immediately past Broxmouth House and moved roughly parallel to the watercourse rather than coming upon the Scots as suggested by Fitz-Payne Fisher's drawing, in which case he would have made a considerable sweep before reaching Campbell of Lawers's brigade. The lithograph, however, cannot be taken too literally for, among its other inconsistencies, Fitz-Payne Fisher placed Dunbar parish kirk far too close to the sea, omitted the English artillery altogether and made the English camp much larger than the Scots one. However much the spoil from quarrying in recent years might have modified (rather than dramatically changed) the conformation of the ground over this part of the battlefield, anyone attempting to follow Cromwell's path from the vicinity of Broxmouth House south-westward while keeping quite close to the Brox Burn, will find no reason to think the original nature of the land would have given him and his troops any major problems underfoot.[12]

In any case, he was not likely to have chosen a difficult route, for it was vital he kept up the momentum of his attacks, but alternatively he would have needed very strong reasons to embark on a wide arc taking in Little Pinkerton, before coming up to the rear and flank of Campbell of Lawers's brigade positioned at the mouth of the Scottish pocket. The core of Cromwell's reserve lay in Pride's infantry brigade and for it to embark on such a wide movement would simply have been unacceptable. On the other hand the shallower route, while undoubtedly faster, involved additional hazards. Above all, it relied on Lambert and Lilburne being able to hold back their Scottish opponents, although Cromwell did have the use of his own cavalry regiment and two companies of Okey's dragoons to help repel any medium-sized cavalry units moving across to stop him.

The other major hazard to Cromwell's intended attack was Lumsden's brigade, battered by Monck but probably reinforced with detachments from Campbell of Lawers's formation, which presently stood eyeball to eyeball with Monck at the Brox Burn. Yet just as Lambert's and Lilburne's cavalry were able to keep their opposite numbers fully engaged, so Monck's brigade, in staying close to Lumsden's inexperienced infantry, prevented them attempting to turn and check Cromwell's progress.

Apart from the continued presence of Monck, the rawness of Lumsden's troops and their considerable number of casualties would not have helped the brigade to attempt such a manoeuvre. In fact, its officers probably would not have realized Cromwell was coming until it was too late, for the cavalry with his reserve would have screened his movements by killing or capturing any Scottish scouts positioned along the burn and, although moving quickly, his experienced troops would doubtless have also made full use of any dead ground between themselves and the enemy. In such fashion Cromwell and the reserve succeeded in covering the one and a half miles of wet, broken grassland from where they had crossed the burn in the vicinity

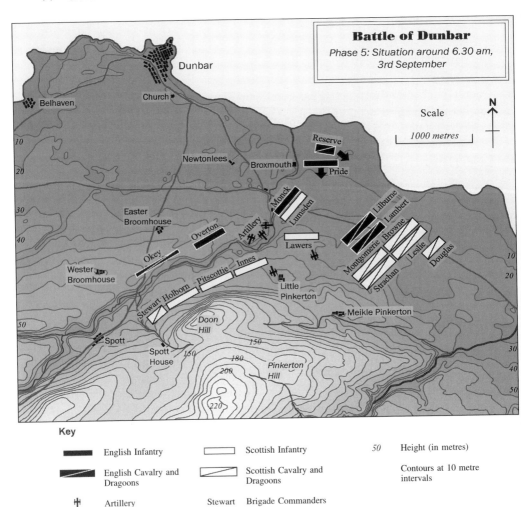

Battle of Dunbar

Phase 5: Situation around 6.30 am,
3rd September

Key

English Infantry

English Cavalry and
Dragoons

Artillery

Scottish Infantry

Scottish Cavalry and
Dragoons

Stewart   Brigade Commanders

50   Height (in metres)

Contours at 10 metre
intervals

of Broxmouth House to come upon Campbell of Lawers's brigade by 7 a.m., just
one hour and a half after Lambert's initial attack against the Scottish cavalry and a
rather shorter interval since Monck's attack upon Lumsden's brigade.

Meanwhile renewed attacks by Lambert and Lilburne had kept the Scottish cavalry
fully occupied while the menace posed by Monck's infantry against Lumsden's
thinned ranks continued to keep that brigade pinned down. Both actions served
to keep Leslie off balance and prevent any substantial movement by his troops in
the pocket from emerging and entering the battle. Conversely, this effectively put
Cromwell in control. He was able to bring the reserve brigade up onto the flank
of Campbell of Lawers's brigade, some of whose men had been detached to bolster
Lumsden's adjacent formation, and although its commanders belatedly attempted
to swing round to face him, the superior English numbers gave Cromwell time to
ensure that once he launched his attacks they would be virtually unstoppable. Pride's
formidable brigade, arguably the best in the English army, included not only his own

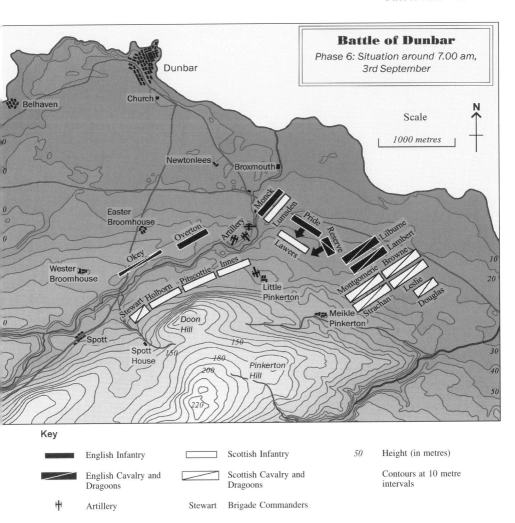

Battle of Dunbar

*Phase 6: Situation around 7.00 am,
3rd September*

Key

English Infantry	Scottish Infantry	*50* Height (in metres)
English Cavalry and Dragoons	Scottish Cavalry and Dragoons	Contours at 10 metre intervals
╫ Artillery	Stewart Brigade Commanders	

foot regiment but Cromwell's and Lambert's, and it also enjoyed the added benefit of having direct cavalry support. Lambert's regiment was the last to come up and Captain Hodgson, who was serving in it, described Cromwell personally lining up its soldiers for their assault – 'The General himself comes to the rear of our regiment and commands it to incline to the left'[13] – so ensuring that Campbell of Lawers's brigade was attacked in both its flank and rear.

At that moment the sun broke through and Hodgson reported he heard Cromwell, when about to unleash his men, shout out in anticipated triumph, 'Now let God arise and his enemies shall be scattered!' At this, snarling drum rolls gave all three regiments the order to charge, the musketeers in front followed closely by their pikemen. Such experienced soldiers needed no reminding that the fate of the battle depended upon them and they went forward with rare purpose, Pride's men apparently with even more savage determination due to either real or imagined cruel usage of their fellow soldiers by the Scots at Brand's Mill the day before.[14] Cromwell watched intently as their muskets barked out and the following pikemen pushed forward into the waiting lines before he roared out, 'I profess they run', at which he laughed uproariously. Cromwell's delight came with the realization that if he could sweep Campbell of Lawers's troops away, the infantry and cavalry brigades filling the pocket would be placed in the greatest danger, having much too little room to wheel about or use their pikes to face his continuing attacks.

He was, in fact, somewhat premature in thinking the Scottish defences had already been breached, for most of Lawers's brigade put up the most obstinate resistance. As Captain Hodgson described it, 'One of the Scots brigades would not yield, though at push of pike and butt end of the musket, until a troop of our horse charged from one end to another of them, and so left them at the mercy of the foot.'[15] Hodgson's account showed the terrifying efficiency of the Ironside cavalry working in tandem with their infantry and although Campbell of Lawers's brigade, mostly armed with firelock pistols, fought with rare courage it was completely destroyed. While Campbell himself was absent, many of his men died where they stood and one of his regiments, commanded by Sir John Haldane of Gleneagles, had its colonel, lieutenant colonel and major all killed.

Such apparent slaughter had predictable and contrasting results on the other units engaged. By then Monck's brigade, led by their commander carrying a spear, had renewed their attacks against Lumsden's brigade, while the English cavalry, duelling with the Scottish horse on the right wing, redoubled their attacks against opponents who, finding themselves unable to protect their infantry or get the better of the heavier English horse, became discouraged. In face of such attacks by Lambert and Lilburne, the numerous cavalry formations on the Scottish right finally broke and ran; some of their survivors fled towards Berwick while more galloped round Doon Hill and made for Haddington and Edinburgh. Cromwell fully recognized the significance of the cavalry's success to his overall plan, writing later that 'The horse in the meantime did with a great deal of courage and spirit beat back all opposition, charging through and through the bodies of the enemies horse.'[16]

With the Scottish cavalry comprehensively driven off the field, the remainder of their army, for the most part in no position to fight effectively, proved no match for the continuing combination of infantry and cavalry attacks mounted by the English veterans. After overcoming Campbell of Lawers's brigade, they moved into the pocket, where other contingents rapidly threw down their arms before attempting to flee. Colonel William Stewart's cavalry furthest to the left were more successful in their flight than most of the infantry who, having discarded their weapons, faced the burn running through its ravine with English dragoons patrolling the other side; most of these were rapidly rounded up and taken prisoner.

As Cromwell had anticipated, once the Scottish resistance at the mouth of the pocket had been broken, the rest of the army's resolve crumbled. So quickly did the end come that the secretary to Cromwell's army, John Rushworth, saw it as one continuous process following Cromwell's decisive flank attack and his troops' penetration deep into the pocket. 'I never beheld a more terrible charge of foot

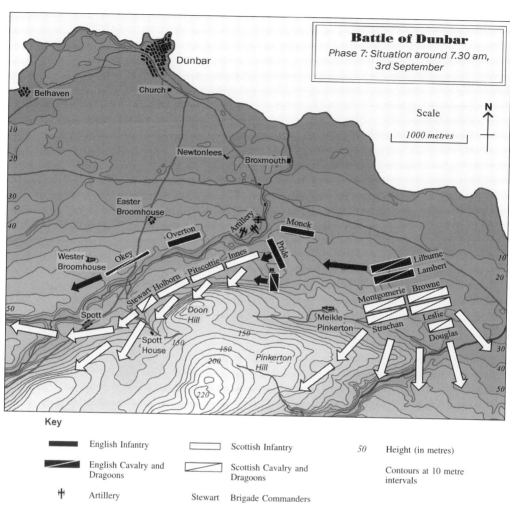

Battle of Dunbar

Phase 7: Situation around 7.30 am, 3rd September

Key

▬▬ English Infantry	▭ Scottish Infantry	*50* Height (in metres)
▨▨ English Cavalry and Dragoons	▱ Scottish Cavalry and Dragoons	Contours at 10 metre intervals
✠ Artillery	Stewart Brigade Commanders	

than was given by our army, our foot alone making the Scots foot give ground for three-quarters of the mile together.'[17]

By 7.30 a.m., before the cows on nearby Lochend Farm had been milked, the proud and more numerous Scottish army that for five weeks had frustrated and harried Cromwell and his Ironsides, bringing them to the brink of defeat, had been completely ruined. It was an amazing victory by a formidable leader whose tactical plan, seemingly against heavy odds, commenced with surprise attacks designed to deny the Scots a third of their strength and concluded with a decisive flank attack supervised personally. It was a victory achieved by using every unit in his small army, where the constricted battlefield at Dunbar worked strongly in his favour by enabling him to continue with his initial attacks and mount his decisive flank attack so quickly that his opponent had little opportunity to recover. As the Scots broke, Cromwell was right to feel elated, and his evident delight was seen in his letters afterwards, but such success could never have been achieved without his subordinate commanders and the spirit of his veteran soldiers who, despite their physical ailments, somehow summoned up the energy to carry out his ambitious and hazardous schemes.

The pride felt by Cromwell for his own regiment came through in one of his subsequent despatches: 'My own regiment under the command of Lieutenant-Colonel Goffe and my Major White did come seasonably in and at push of pike did repel the stoutest regiment the enemy had there merely with the courage the Lord was pleased to give; which proved a great amazement to the residue of their foot.'[18] In a report to William Lenthall he duly gave more general credit to his men: 'both your chief commanders and others in their several places, and soldiers also, were [actuated] with as much courage as ever hath been seen in any action since this war.' However, being Cromwell, he did not allow himself to become too carried away or let other individuals detract too much from his own success. 'I know they look not to be named and therefore I forbear particulars!' In his unique capacity as the Lord's personal sword-bearer, while Cromwell was happy to credit God with making the Scots 'as stubble to our swords', he knew the English Parliament would have been left in no doubt as to whom they owed their success. However, with Charles II still King of Scotland, victory at Dunbar did not mark the end of the military campaign, but a massive step towards Scotland's complete subjection.

In the case of Leslie, with victory seemingly within his grasp, he had allowed his army to become vulnerable to a fast-thinking and fast-moving opponent, just as the Engagers had done some two years before. The south of Scotland was now likely to fall into Cromwell's hands, but there was still a chance that a sizeable proportion of those who had scattered would rejoin the colours, even though virtually all their equipment had been lost and many new levies would have to be found and trained. While Leslie made a breakneck dash from Dunbar over the Lammermuirs to Edinburgh, no doubt speculating about his own uncertain future, he would have been less than human if he had not recalled the recent sight of a failing English army plodding painfully along from Musselburgh to Dunbar and wondered whether, in fact, he would ever be given the chance to lead another Scottish army against Cromwell and, if so, what might be his chances of victory.

Whatever forces Scotland succeeded in reassembling and whoever was chosen to direct them, Leslie would have been in no doubt that the struggle would go on.

Part III

Fruits of Victory

Chapter 9

Capture and Exploitation

We did say to one another, we knew not what to do.
(Oliver Cromwell, *Writings*)

For Cromwell, defeating the enemy on the battlefield was only half the task. Their loss of cohesion had to be exploited fully[1] and his victory made total, helping to bring the war to an end. Before his pursuing troopers could spread out across the countryside he ordered them to close up and sing the 113th Psalm with its opening and final sentences of 'Praise the Lord'. Certainly no Puritan soldier could refuse to give thanks to his Lord for the victory, particularly at Cromwell's ordering, but the pause to sing that relatively short psalm also brought the additional advantage that the party would, as Cromwell intended, grow large enough to embark on a disciplined and more effective pursuit of the fleeing enemy. This was an activity to Cromwell's taste and his messenger reported 'that our horse and foot pursued even the whole army and cut down and killed near four thousand, following them as far as Haddington, being about eight miles from the place, and Hacker's regiment pursued beyond Haddington, *our general himself* being in the pursuit.'[2] The pioneer English newspaper *Mercurius Politicus* put the total casualties inflicted higher still at between 4,000 and 5,000, along with the generally agreed figure of 10,000 soldiers captured.[3]

The number of casualties suffered by your opponent is, of course, a most important aspect of any battlefield success, especially if the victor's losses prove to be light. This was certainly the case with the English at Dunbar, although they must surely have been above the minuscule total of 'not twenty men' put out by Cromwell. For the vanquished, in addition to the human cost came the penalty of losing scarce military resources together with the immense difficulties over replacing them. Cromwell told Speaker Lenthall his men had captured the whole Scottish baggage train of 15,000 arms, powder and bullets, together with all their artillery, great and small – thirty guns.[4] During the next year the Scots would have particular cause to regret the loss of their artillery. As visual evidence of his success Cromwell sent 200 captured Scottish colours to London's Westminster Hall to join those already hanging there from his and Lambert's earlier victory at Preston against the Engagers.

But however determined and successful the English might have been in their pursuit following the battle, after their previous losses and extreme exertions of the night before they could never have expected to destroy the whole Scottish army. Inflicting some 5,000 casualties and taking twice as many prisoners from a force about 21,000 strong was remarkable enough, but nevertheless, some time after nine o'clock, by using a string of horses and riding them as hard as he could, Leslie succeeded in reaching Edinburgh to ensure that the fight would go on. There he would be joined by about 4,000 survivors, chiefly from the cavalry. Old Leven, Leslie's nominal superior, also escaped. He was unlikely to have taken an active part in directing the battle – Carlyle said he was there only as a volunteer without command – but being 'not so light of movement'[5] as Leslie he did not reach Edinburgh until two in the afternoon. However much Leslie might be out of favour, due to Leven's advanced age and in view of his physical limitations, there seemed no chance of him being reinstated as field commander of the Scottish forces.

While the Scots were faced with the problems over their future leadership and the mammoth task of raising yet another field army, the number of Scottish prisoners was destined to give the English especial difficulties too. In view of Cromwell's earlier ruthlessness in Ireland towards prisoners, and the turn of events with the Scottish prisoners after Dunbar, the full facts here are essential. In the first place, it is fair to say that such high totals, following the wholesale and sudden surrender of the Scottish army, represented a situation for which the Ironsides were not equipped. Cromwell wrote to the lord president of the Council of State about the so-called 'Dunbar drove', where the English soldiers ended up capturing men as readily as fishermen filling their nets with shoals of herring: 'We are put to exceeding trouble, though it be an effect of abundant mercy, with the numerousness of our prisoners.'[6] Traditionally one would have expected a higher proportion to have been killed: there were far too many to exchange and, as Scottish patriots, they would not be willing to serve in the English army, nor could they be allowed to rejoin the Scottish forces. During the earlier Civil Wars prisoners had been frequently released on parole after giving their word that they would never again take up arms against their opponents, but on this occasion Cromwell seemed unwilling to believe any such undertaking if made by Scotsmen. A major problem with so many prisoners was that Cromwell had barely enough food for his own troops, let alone a further 10,000 men, and the number of guards required from his small and sickly army also threatened to hamper his future military operations.

On the day after the battle Cromwell therefore decided to release between four and five thousand of 'the poorer physical specimens, those almost starved, sick and wounded',[7] who could not be used for some considerable time, if ever, against him. In this regard he also showed mercy for the wounded still remaining on the battlefield and towards the citizens of Dunbar by permitting them to drive carts out and take back any Scottish soldiers lying there for treatment. There were strong reasons for such an act, particularly its good effects upon the local people and as a demonstration of his genuine concern for fighting men, but in any case their numbers would have been relatively small since some would already have been despatched by his soldiers and the survivors were likely to be long-term convalescents at best. This left the larger portion of able-bodied men, whom Cromwell told Sir Arthur Hesilrige, his governor at Newcastle, would be sent to him under the escort of four troops from Colonel Hacker's regiment. They would be delivered into Hesilrige's care to be used as directed by the English Council of State. In reality, under the customs of war at that time the English had no right to remove soldiers from Scotland who had fought for their native country. Cromwell did not feel himself subject to such restrictions. There was even a report by Sir Edward Walker that, in an act of gallantry, he authorized 1,000 of the prisoners to be sent 'as a present' to the Countess of Winton in East Lothian, although it is not certain whether these were ever delivered to her or if so, whether they were subsequently included with those that were sent south.

Such a directive, together with the other arrangements subsequently made by Hesilrige, would, of course, be unjustifiable under the contemporary rules of war and infinitely more so under present-day Geneva Conventions, but if the Scots had won at Dunbar and the English had surrendered in a similar fashion the Ironsides would probably have received little better treatment. Cromwell's main intention was to remove the possibility that such prisoners would continue the war. On 9 September, he wrote a second letter to Hesilrige saying, 'I hope your Northern Guests are come to you by this time. I pray you let humanity be exercised towards them: I am persuaded it will be comely. Let the officers be kept at Newcastle, some sent to Lynn, some to Chester.'[8] The tone is ironic and the request somewhat lukewarm, although this second instruction to Hesilrige might have suggested that Cromwell did not altogether trust the governor's capacity for human kindness but, in any case, Cromwell cannot be held directly responsible for the terrible sufferings that such men experienced on their way to Newcastle. Hesilrige was also contacted by the English Council of State, who were as merciless as Cromwell in their intended disposal of the prisoners, originally instructing Hesilrige to deliver 900 men by 19 September to Samuel Clarke, a ship's master, to be transported to Virginia and sold there to Joshua Foote and John Beck, with a further 200 to be sent to Isaac le Guy, also in Virginia. A further 2,300 were to be sent for military service in Ireland, except Highlanders because of their 'affinity to the Irish', and a final 300 were intended for military service in France.[9] Including some 200 officers detached from the marching column, the Council's totals amounted to just under 4,000 men, close to Cromwell's own figures for the prisoners that he reckoned set off from Dunbar. In fact, the numbers for such tasks would be dramatically reduced. In partial mitigation, apart from their lack of regard for the prisoners, Colonel Hacker's troops had no experience of the logistics involved in marshalling over 4,000 prisoners along a ninety-mile journey, men who, despite Cromwell's instructions about the officers, seemed to have been separated from them already and therefore lacked official spokesmen to protect their interests or representatives to oversee their discipline. Before setting off, some of the natural leaders had already managed to escape and when the column had covered the thirty-mile journey to Berwick without food of any kind, a number of the prisoners fell down and refused to move unless they could eat something. The troopers' rough response was to pistol thirty to death on the spot and order the column to resume its southward march. Hacker's inability to distribute any food at all defies explanation and the column was chased along pitilessly until they arrived at Morpeth where, after nearly eight days on the road and seventy-five miles from their starting point, the prisoners were driven into a large walled area where cabbages were grown. There, to the ready amusement of their guards, the starving men bolted down the cabbages, muddy roots and all. By this time, being close to Newcastle, they came under Hesilrige's direct care who, in a subsequent letter to the English Council of State whitewashing his part in what had unquestionably become a human disaster, described their parlous condition and the immense pains he had avowedly taken to assist them: 'In their need they poysoned their bodies; for as they were coming from thence to Newcastle I put them into the greatest church in the town and the next morning when I sent them to Durham about seven score were sick they being told into the great cathedral church they could not count them to more than 3,000.'

In such fashion Hesilrige acknowledged that a thousand or more had already been lost, either from escaping, being executed or dying from disease hastened by starvation and exhaustion. Hesilrige maintained he sent them a daily supply of bread and milk from Newcastle and the neighbouring towns. He then removed the sick from the cathedral to the bishop's castle next door where they were reputedly given pottage, with oatmeal, beef and cabbages – and as 'I dare confidently say, there was never the like care taken for any such number of prisoners that ever were in England.'[10] Notwithstanding, many of them still died, including some who Hesilrige said in a show of bestial behaviour had killed each other: 'if any had good clothes, he that wanted, if he was able, would strangle the other and put on his clothes.' Such 'internal' murders were very convenient to help him justify losses on the march. Hesilrige's subsequent account about the remaining 3,000 men was remarkably detailed, a fact of which the bluff governor was only too well aware. 'Gentlemen, you cannot but think strange this long preamble and to wonder which the matter will be; in short it's this. Of the 3,000 prisoners 1,600 are dead and buried nor can any account hold true long because they still dye daily, and doubtless, so they will, so long as any remain in prison.'[11] The survivors mentioned by Hesilrige at this time numbered just 600 fit men (mostly Highlanders) and 500 sick.

On learning of the losses the Council of State were themselves not sure what to do with the survivors and the problems facing the remaining men were by no means at an end. Hesilrige no longer had anything like 1,100 fit men for Virginia and New England, and by the end of October he had only been able to send 350 men to Samuel Clarke to be moved down to London. Many of these fell sick on the way and by 7 November the rest were apparently still in the infamous 'pest-house' at Blackwall or on hulks in the Thames awaiting ships. Although Clarke was made to answer a charge of maltreating his prisoners, this came to nothing and in the end just 150 prisoners were sent to Augustine Walker, the skipper of the New England ship *Unity*, for shipment to a New England ironworks whose directors were John Beck and Joshua Foote. The voyage was due to take about six weeks; the *Unity* was not a large vessel and following their imprisonment between 10 and 20 per cent of the survivors could be expected to die on the voyage. In fact, a third were subsequently unaccounted for.

Walker sold the men for between £20 and £30 each: fifteen to twenty-five went to a sawmill on the Piscatagua river in Maine where Beck had a major interest, while sixty-two went to John Gifford, the agent for the Saugus ironworks at Lynn, Massachusetts. The rest were sold to other residents in the nearby town of York where, like other indentured servants, the length of service required before obtaining their freedom was seven years.[12] Happily, in the New World the prisoners were not badly treated and in the case of the majority (who went to the Saugus ironworks) their employer built a house for every four of them with some acres of ground round about, where they were required to work three days for their master with four days for themselves with the promise that 'as soon as they can repay the money laid out for them he will set them at liberty.'[13] Those in Maine were given land worth £25 on their release and a proportion became successful farmers.

Hesilrige had also allocated relatively small numbers for specialist tasks, forty or so as indentured servants, another handful to work at the salt pans at (South) Sheels, twelve weavers to be kept at Newcastle 'to begin the trade of linen cloth like unto the Scotch cloth' and forty to be sold as general labourers.[14] In his account of the prisoners, apart from those set to work as described, Hesilrige listed 30 shot escaping, 1,600 dying on the march, 500 'missing' between Berwick and Newcastle, as well as the 1,100 men 'sick and fit' at Durham. From the 1,100 'sick and fit' some 500 were sent to Ireland to serve in the British army there and in 1651 the rest were ordered to France, but after spending a protracted period in a Tynemouth Jail, the fittest – probably something like 100 – were sent to Barbados.[15]

One will never know the full truth about how so many of the men who had set off from Dunbar perished. Without doubt their early treatment had been barbaric and had contributed to the casualty levels of about 60 per cent (compared with a mortality of 30 per cent suffered by the British prisoners of the Japanese during the Second World War engaged on constructing the infamous Burma Railway[16]). However, by early 1651, apart from the relatively small number engaged on specialist tasks in England, together with a few sickly individuals still being treated, some of whom were subsequently put on forced labour to help drain the fens at King's Lynn, the majority of the remaining prisoners had been sent overseas.

Whether Cromwell had intended this to happen or not, events undoubtedly worked to his advantage: the new Scottish army presently being levied for service against him would contain very few recruits from those he had originally taken prisoner at Dunbar.

Cromwell's attempts to 'knock out' the opposing Scottish army were, of course, in accordance with his aim of ending the war quickly. To have any chance of this he had to catch the Scots before they could reassemble their survivors, reconstruct their defences or recruit more levies. Accordingly, he immediately despatched the indefatigable Lambert with seven cavalry and one infantry regiment to seize Edinburgh while he, with the remainder of the army under his command, captured Edinburgh's port of Leith three days later, thus ensuring his army's new requirements for resupply, although Lambert did not prove quick enough to catch Leslie, who had moved on with about 4,000 soldiers, together with the Kirk's civilian leaders, to the fortress of Stirling. Lambert succeeded, however, in taking Edinburgh's defences without a fight, with the notable exception of the castle which, from its dominant position over the city, defied the English for a further two and a half months. By occupying Edinburgh and Leith, Cromwell gained the major base and port he had long been seeking in the heart of Scotland, along with the strong likelihood of obtaining other food supplies from the fertile plain lying between Edinburgh and Glasgow. He made his headquarters at Edinburgh, just outside the city's walls in the Earl of Moray's splendid house along the Canongate, while he based the main part of his army in the vicinity of nearby Holyrood House. Although Leslie had eluded him so far, Cromwell still hoped to make a swift move west to crack open the fortifications at Stirling and then, by using its river bridge, cross the Forth and bring the war rapidly to an end.

Whatever their leader's eagerness, the army required an interval in which to recover and he was obliged to give them a week off duties. During this time he opened communications with Sir Walter Dundas – in command of the castle in place of Leven – calling upon him to surrender. Dundas refused[17] but on 12 September, as soon as his army was able, leaving Colonel Overton with four infantry regiments to garrison the capital, Cromwell made for Stirling. As so often during that season it rained heavily during the journey and due to the poor conditions underfoot Cromwell was forced to send his heaviest guns back to Edinburgh. Nonetheless, after four days he and his army stood before Stirling's walls, where his messenger summoned its garrison to submit. Although Stirling's defences were far from complete, Leslie refused and Cromwell, without an adequate siege train and with his agent William Rowe telling him about the numbers of supplementary forces available to the Scots, allegedly adding up to 25,000 men, decided against attempting an assault. Although his request for further reinforcements from the Council of State had resulted in some men coming from Newcastle, Cromwell's army was still only 13,000 strong and he was in no position to risk the likely casualties from a direct assault or, even worse, court the prospect of failure. In any event, Stirling stood on the south bank of the Forth and before moving further north he would have to mount an additional attack to secure its bridge. Cromwell ordered the army back to Linlithgow (about fifteen miles west of Edinburgh) which he fortified and garrisoned before subsequently returning to Edinburgh.

Leslie's occupation of Stirling, whose castle high on its volcanic stump bears a strong resemblance to Edinburgh's, and his strengthening of the defences there, posed a real threat to Cromwell's attempts to complete the conquest of Scotland during 1650. In any event, he needed to consolidate his gains over an increasingly resentful country where several guerrilla forces had come into being and where the weather conditions were deteriorating; consequently, in spite of gathering ships and men for a crossing of the Firth of Forth, on 27 September Cromwell cancelled the operation.

Significant elements from his small army had already been required to garrison certain fortified houses and castles around Edinburgh and used to eliminate the so-called moss-troopers operating in the south-east that threatened his lines of communication. These small bands of horsemen based in strongholds, including castles, had become expert at hit and run raids against soft targets, particularly the English food convoys. Over 1,600 English soldiers, for instance, were involved besieging Dirleton Castle in East Lothian occupied by the moss-trooper Captain Watt, who held out until early November when General Monck fired mortar shells into the interior and, upon its surrender, released sixty prisoners and their horses before shooting Captain Watt by firing squad. Two of the best-known leaders of moss-troopers at this time were Augustine Hoffman, a German ex-mercenary, and a local commander, Sandy Kerr.[18] Cromwell, who executed any of his own soldiers found plundering, took a very tough line with such guerrilla fighters, together with those that protected them, saying, 'I will require life for life, and a plenary satisfaction for the goods of those parishes and places where the fact should be committed unless they shall discover and produce the offender.'[19] By the end of the year the moss-troopers had been virtually destroyed in actions which Cromwell found doubly useful, helping to keep his soldiers alert, rather than allowing them to stagnate in garrisons, where many had wasted little time in marrying Scottish girls. However, Hoffman was still free in December, for on the night of the 13th, accompanied by 120 riders, he succeeded in entering Edinburgh through the Canongate port before galloping up the High Street to the castle, where he left ammunition before breaking out again half an hour later.

Just as during the period before Dunbar, whatever his military initiatives, Cromwell continued to wage a concurrent war of propaganda to take advantage of any major divisions in the Scottish leadership. Its three main competing groups – the ruling (moderate) Kirk party, the king and the extreme believers – gave him obvious scope for mischief-making: immediately after the battle, for instance, he wrote to Hesilrige revealing his appreciation of the new situation: 'Surely, its probable the Kirk has done their do. I believe their King will set upon his own score now, whereas he will find many friends.'[20]

On 9 October, having learned of an attempted coup on behalf of the king, Cromwell took the opportunity to write to the Scottish Committee of Estates attributing to Charles II responsibility for all Scotland's problems: 'And we are persuaded those difficulties in which you have involved yourselves – by espousing your King's interest have occasioned your rejecting these overtures which, with a Christian affection, were offered to you before any blood was spilt, or your people suffered damage by us.'[21] In an attempt to turn the screw further, he moved his army (now reinforced) from Edinburgh to Linlithgow and then to Glasgow, where he tried to win favour with the clergy, for he knew that Colonels Strachan and Ker – both fanatical kirkmen – had also been seeking their support. While in Glasgow Cromwell received reports of a likely attempt by Leslie to relieve Edinburgh Castle and therefore on 14 October he returned to the Scottish capital. The rumour proved unfounded but it served to demonstrate how Cromwell could move his army across southern Scotland at will.

Cromwell's communication with the Scottish Committee of Estates imputing all blame for the war to Charles II was astutely done, for after their defeat at Dunbar they had decided the king must be brought further under their control by purging his court.[22] As a result Charles and his traditional supporters, such as the Gordons and the Earls of Atholl and Airlie, plotted to place him in control of northern Scotland, but their proposed arrangements for a coup proved far too complicated and they misfired; on 6 October Charles, after riding over forty miles that day, was discovered alone, hiding in a humble cottage near the Earl of Airlie's seat at Cortachy Castle, by General Montgomerie and 600 horse sent out by the Committee of Estates. The shambolic affair was ironically dubbed 'the Start' and Charles was taken back to Perth and obliged to make a humiliating apology to Chancellor Loudon for his conduct in it, although it did not result in the chaos for which Cromwell could have hoped.

At around the same time Cromwell's informants were aware of another challenge to the Kirk party, this time from the two religious fanatics Colonels Archibald Strachan and Gilbert Ker, whom the Committee of Estates had appointed to raise much-needed levies from the west of Scotland. Their response had been to recruit an independent army of their own, the so-called Western Association, and on 2 October they produced a Remonstrance, followed by a second fourteen days later, in which they accused Charles II of failing to repent or expel 'all disaffected and profane persons' from the forces, with the result that at Dunbar Scotland had been duly visited by 'the wrath of God'.[23] Although the Remonstrants were also committed to expel Cromwell from Scotland, they had no intention of invading England, where they accepted the rule of the Independents, but it was their refusal to acknowledge the king or serve under Leslie that represented a challenge the ruling Kirk party could not ignore. By mid-November, after striking an agreement with the powerful and traditionally Royalist families in the north-east, it despatched General Robert Montgomerie to take over the Remonstrants' army, now commanded by Ker. (Strachan had already been confined for favouring a reconciliation with Cromwell.) In the circumstances, Ker realized his only chance of survival was to regain favour by defeating Cromwell's forces in Lanarkshire, but faced by the incomparable

Lambert he had little chance of such an achievement and after his plans for a surprise attack failed he was wounded and taken prisoner, and the Western army was destroyed.

Whatever challenges the ruling Kirk party faced from the king and the Western Association, after Lambert destroyed the latter's army Cromwell's hopes for political chaos receded. In fact, his menacing presence brought about greater Scottish unity and on 14 December, just two days after a meeting of the Church Commissioners in Perth, it resolved to readmit Royalists and ex-Engagers – provided they humbly apologized for their past shortcomings – into what promised to become a national army. Such insistence on public repentance, however, remained a deterrent to some and it caused John Middleton, the Engagers' senior cavalry general, never to forget, or forgive, the humiliation of having to make his apologies dressed in sackcloth.[24] In such circumstances the levying of a more representative army was bound to take time while the effects of the king's growing role in Scotland's military preparations were yet to become clear.

Meanwhile, Cromwell continued in his attempts to complete his conquest. Signs that his own reputation in England had been enhanced by his victory at Dunbar became evident when a medal was minted to commemorate it, featuring on one side a bust of Cromwell surrounded by the words 'The Lord of Hosts', and Oxford University invited him to be its chancellor. To Cromwell, however, neither token of greater recognition appeared important compared with defeat of the Scots. His immediate military target was the capture of Edinburgh Castle and following a number of verbal exchanges with its governor, Walter Dundas, he brought up Derbyshire miners to sap its walls: they found its rock remarkably difficult to penetrate and therefore it was not until 12 December that Cromwell was able to mount a serious bombardment with heavy guns shipped in from Leith. Although their shot did not prove particularly effective against its massive defences, Dundas had already been discouraged by Lambert's defeat of the Western Association's army and he finally offered to treat with Cromwell. After prolonged negotiations, which included generous terms for the garrison, agreement upon the castle's surrender was finally reached on 24 December.

Despite this success Cromwell still had far to go before his conquest of Scotland was complete, although a week after the castle's fall Robert Baillie, Scotland's shrewd commentator on its national affairs, emphasized the severity of his country's problems following its defeat at Dunbar. 'Our standing forces against his imminent invasion, few, weak and inconsiderable: our Kirk, State, Army full of divisions and jealousies, the body of our people be-south [of the river] Forth spoiled, and near starving; they be-north Forth extremely ill-used by a handful of our own: many inclining to treat and agree with Cromwell, without care either of King or Covenant. What the end of it all shall be the Lord knows.'[25]

Whatever the dark, if not desperate, tone of Baillie upon Scotland's misfortunes, by the end of 1650 Cromwell's aim to teach Scotland the error of recognizing Charles II as its king remained unfulfilled, and Charles II's own position appeared likely to grow stronger. Yet, without his victory at Dunbar, instead of occupying all Scotland south of the Forth and confidently hoping to complete his conquest during 1651, the best Cromwell could have hoped for would have been garrisoning the town's small and insignificant port.

During the coming year the longer-term effects of the battle would prove even more significant for both sides.

Chapter 10

Towards Full Conquest

One we must Protector call
From whom the King of Heaven protect us all.
(Seventeenth-century anonymous Scottish poem)

Cromwell's preparations to cross the Forth and his capture of Edinburgh Castle were powerful reminders of his continuing determination to complete the conquest of Scotland. If the Scots were to have a chance of successfully opposing him they had to further relax their rules of eligibility for joining the army and recruit able-bodied men from wherever they could still be found.

An instance of this occurred on 20 December when it was decided that colonels appointed to raise and train regiments should include not only Royalists and Engagers, but even men who had previously fought with Montrose against the Covenanters. Another major step towards a more unified response to Cromwell's invasions came with the coronation of Charles II on New Year's Day, which, in accordance with long tradition, took place at Scone. However, the ceremony also revealed the Kirk party's reluctance to cede power, for although Charles was crowned he was not anointed and, having been obliged to restate his intention to uphold the Covenant, he was then forced to sit through a sermon lecturing him on the Kirk's pivotal position in the state. Any institution that felt compelled so to emphasize its power was clearly in danger of losing it and, as Samuel Gardiner was later to observe in his measured fashion, from this time stricter Covenanters, such as Strachan and others, would never again grasp 'the reins of government and mould armies at their pleasure. Their impracticable zeal, their intolerance of contradiction, would still produce martyrs, in some of whom it is hard to draw the line between criminal and hero; but they could no more produce men who claimed to be statesmen and generals.'[1] For the ruling moderates the use of Royalist colonels to help raise the Scottish army had already signalled change in Scotland's military policy. No earlier Stuart king would have stayed on the defensive for as long as Leslie had done during the previous year and, prior to Dunbar, Charles II had in fact recommended more aggressive action before being removed from the area of hostilities by the Kirk officials. By early 1651 such high-handed behaviour was no longer conceivable and, in any case, the declared monarch of both England and Scotland was sure to view Royalist conspiracies in England in a way very different from David Leslie.

During the first half of 1651 the crown's strength continued to grow at the expense of the Kirk party. In March, the Scottish Parliament admitted Royalists onto its committee responsible for managing the army[2] and in May, after the Act of Classes was finally rescinded, Royalists were again eligible to assume public posts. This change of attitude was further illustrated soon afterwards when the Church's General Assembly voted in favour of depriving extreme ministers, such as James Guthrie and Patrick Gillespie, of their livings, and also condemned the Western Remonstrance. At the same time Scotland's latest military preparations were going ahead: under Leven's nominal command some 18,000 recruits were being raised and trained by David Leslie in various locations, both near Stirling and in Fife, although as yet there had been little opportunity to obtain an adequate amount of new equipment.

The veteran English army lying snug in its winter quarters at Musselburgh had no such problems over its training and equipment and, with plentiful stocks of food to hand, it stood ready to carry out Cromwell's directives. However, on both sides any projected military operations were severely hampered by the high winds, sleet and snow of a Scottish winter, although this did not stop either side from trying: in mid-January a force of 800 Scottish cavalry left Stirling with the intention of seizing Linlithgow but the attempt failed. A possible rejoinder by Monck on the 18th was also thwarted when, after crossing the Forth with 1,500 men for an intended attack on Burntisland in Fife, he was unable to land his force in the adverse weather conditions. As a result the English Council of State approved the considerable expenditure required for the building, in London and Newcastle, of fifty flat-bottomed boats, each to be manned by a captain and five seamen.

By the end of January the weather relented somewhat and on 4 February Cromwell led the English army out. He marched westward to Linlithgow, then Kilsyth, before turning north in an optimistic attempt to cross the Forth just west of Stirling. Apart from their cavalry scouts, the bulk of the Scottish forces wisely stayed in their bases and, faced with deteriorating weather, the English turned back, discouraged by the fact that the conditions caused Cromwell to fall ill with a severe form of ague, from which he did not recover fully until early June, thus giving the Scots much-needed breathing space in which to rebuild their forces.

The English, however, continued to mount a number of smaller-scale operations during this time, chiefly under the leadership of General Monck. On 13 February he moved against the formidable castle of Tantallon with its massive straight wall closing off a small promontory, which was held by moss-troopers under Captain Alexander Seaton. Monck took with him two regiments of foot, six great guns and a mortar. Although Seaton burnt the little town lying in front of the castle walls to give his men a clear field of fire, this did not prevent the English guns from battering against the castle's massive outer wall until it tumbled into the dry ditch in front. Upon this

Seaton requested a parley, which Monck refused, and after eight days, on 21 February, Seaton surrendered, emerging with fewer than 100 fellow defenders, 12 horses and 16 assorted guns. The prisoners were led captive to Edinburgh before being sent south to an English prison.[3] On 1 April Monck and his troops took Blackness Castle, situated on the south side of the Forth, just two miles from Linlithgow. This had provided an excellent base for Scottish raiding parties and indeed a month earlier a considerable force of cavalry had been landed there. Monck's operation was characteristically well planned and he used the navy to bombard it from the seaward side while he besieged it from the land.

But in reality, such limited successes barely dented the Scottish defences; they not only retained the fortress of Stirling but kept control over the south bank of the Firth of Forth from the Queensferry narrows eastwards. In any case, Cromwell had other concerns, for during his continuing absence from England Royalist sympathies had grown. On 29 March Thomas Coke, an agent involved in preparing risings against the Commonwealth, was captured and to save his life he revealed a mass of information about planned uprisings involving almost every English county. Government troops were despatched without delay to the potential trouble spots and many of those involved were quickly rounded up. But it gave Cromwell a clear signal that he must complete his task in Scotland as quickly as possible and return to his seat of power, even though the efficiency of the Commonwealth's military response had dealt an even greater blow to Charles II's hopes in England.

In April Cromwell had regained his health sufficiently to prevent a sizeable Scottish skirmishing party, under Colonel Robert Montgomerie, from taking Linlithgow and going on to recruit in the west for the new Scottish army. Cromwell's response was remarkable; in a singular show of strength he took the whole of his army – now some 16,000 to 18,000 strong – out of its quarters in Musselburgh and led it on a rapid march to Glasgow, forty-seven miles away. There he stayed for eleven days conversing with Scottish divines from both the town and university to such an effect that, when he left, the town authorities were in considerable turmoil as to their loyalties (as he had intended they should be). After marching back to Edinburgh he showed off his ample reserves of food by distributing a week's supply to the whole army.

A less dramatic but possibly more significant reaction to Montgomerie's raids in the west was for the English to withdraw many of their smaller and more vulnerable garrisons, such as those at Hamilton and Dumfries, from danger. This enabled them to concentrate their forces better for any major operations in the future, although historian John Grainger believes the decision represented a deliberate bait to tempt Charles II into moving south.[4]

For the Scots even to be considering such action suggested a considerable military recovery on their part, assisted by their appointment of commanders on the basis of ability rather than primarily for party considerations. Although David Leslie and Leven remained Charles II's senior commanders, the ex-Engager John Middleton was made lieutenant general of horse, assisted here by leading Covenanters Robert Montgomerie and Sir John Browne as his major generals. James Holborn, whose political sympathies were close to those of Cromwell's sectaries, was appointed lieutenant general of infantry, with the moderate Covenanter Walter Scott of Pitscottie (who had been at Dunbar with Leslie) and Thomas Dalyell of the Binns (who had served with Monro in Ulster) as his two major generals. While more representative, so many generals undoubtedly made the command structure top-heavy and the shortage of equipment was still a major problem: the English newspaper, *Mercurius Politicus*, for instance, put the Scottish army's total artillery at no more than '14 guns, great and small'.[5]

As a consequence the Scottish forces still appeared no match in open battle for Cromwell's veterans, now reinforced to almost the same numerical level, with their larger proportion of small arms and superior artillery further supplemented by the guns of the English navy. Such superiority counted for less, however, if the Scots chose to stay in their redoubtable fortress at Stirling, while positioning other formations to block any English attempts to cross the Forth. Keeping to such a strategy even put time on the side of the Scots, and although the English continued to occupy southern Scotland, Cromwell, as leader of a radical and far from universally popular administration, could not afford to be tied up in Scotland for another campaigning season. In early June *Mercurius Politicus* voiced serious concerns in London about the delays to his campaigning during 1651 – 'The beauty of the summer is passing away very fast and we are not yet upon any action'[6] – and there even seemed to be a growing belief that, as W S Douglas put it, if Cromwell did not act quickly the chances were that the cradle of the infant Commonwealth would be rocked to some purpose.[7] Whether there was genuine cause for so much concern, the English military offensive against Scotland needed to be speedily renewed and pursued to much greater effect.

Two leading London doctors were summoned to Edinburgh to help restore Cromwell's health, but by the time they reached the Scottish capital he finally seemed close to recovery. There were indications of this when, at the end of May, he promoted Lambert and Monck to full generals and made Colonel Richard Green, his liaison officer to the fleet, a major general, an appointment that appeared to indicate what might be his best offensive option, for he was still reluctant to assault Stirling directly (whose defences had been further improved) and risk the probable high casualties. Cromwell had already received his fifty flat-bottomed boats and he knew the Scots had too few men to defend the whole of the Fife coast against a seaborne attack from boats that could be beached anywhere. On the other hand, to mount a landing as far east as Fife meant dividing his army, thus offering the Scots the opportunity of moving across from their positions near Stirling to destroy the English bridgeheads before they could be built up, or, alternatively, offering them the chance to send their main army southward into England while the English were engaged on their northern landings.

Cromwell's agents were sure to have informed him that the Scots had been able to assemble only six weeks' food supplies, thus giving them strong reasons to make the first offensive moves. Such reports proved correct, although it was not until 28 June that the Scots moved out of Stirling to occupy a strong position in the Torwood, just six miles to the south of the city. To Cromwell this might have appeared as a possible staging post for a march south into England or for an attack on Edinburgh, and therefore he moved his army from its camp in the Pentland Hills with the intention of seeking out the Scottish army and defeating it as he had at Dunbar. He moved across to Linlithgow and then on to Falkirk, only to discover, as in the previous year, that the Scottish positions were too strong to attack. After a series of manoeuvres and counter-manoeuvres, by 7 July Cromwell had crossed in front of the Scottish army to reach Glasgow, whereupon Leslie responded by moving from the Torwood to another powerful position at Kilsyth, where he could block a series of fords that Lambert had discovered might be used to cross the Forth. When, in reply, the English moved halfway between Falkirk and Linlithgow, Leslie returned to the Torwood. To Cromwell it was like 1650 all over again and, after Leslie's defeat at Dunbar, there seemed far less chance of him risking an open battle with the English.

Next Cromwell attempted to provoke Leslie and Charles II into a fight by attacking Callendar House near Falkirk as he had done at Red Hall the year before. After bombarding it all day with their great guns, the English stormed in, killing sixty-one men including Lieutenant Galbraith, the governor of the garrison – but the Scots still did not move. Despite the king's presence Cromwell probably had only limited hopes of his attack on Callendar House bringing his opponents into the open. On the other hand, it would undoubtedly serve to divert their leaders' attention while he acted on the option he had already favoured, namely crossing over the Firth of Forth towards Fife.

For this he used Colonel Daniel's regiment, which was garrisoned at Leith. It moved as if to meet up with the main English army but, after being joined by four troops of Colonel Overton's horse, the augmented force stepped into the assembled flat boats and moved across the Firth at its narrowest point to occupy North Queensferry. The manoeuvre was accomplished before the Scots could react and continued during 19–20 July: the overall English commander, John Lambert, by using every available vessel in the area, succeeded in sending more soldiers across until he raised the strength of his bridgehead to a considerable 5,000 men. In response Leslie did not move his main army eastward, preferring to despatch a contingent of 4,000 soldiers who, under the command of General Holborn and Sir John Browne, were far closer to Queensferry, although once again he seemed to underestimate the offensive power of Cromwell's army. Holborn was ordered to check Lambert, whose path northward along the small Inverkeithing peninsula overlooking Queensferry required him to cross a series of steep ridges well suited to defence. Holborn would have done well to dig in on one of these, but he contented himself with using his forces as a covering screen. Lambert's response was as brilliant as ever: by hiding most of his troops on a reverse slope, he lured the Scots into the attack and responded with a devastating reply from his own right flank. The engagement lasted less than half an hour; General Holborn quickly fled and Sir John Browne was to die of the wound he received there.

As at Dunbar, the Highland formations fought with amazing bravery: 800 MacLeans and 700 Buchanans died where they stood; many MacLeans cheerfully gave their lives to protect their chieftain, Sir Hector MacLean, shouting as they stepped forward to likely death, 'Another for Sir Hector!' Lambert pursued the broken forces ferociously for six miles, at the conclusion of which he had killed 2,000 men and taken a further 1,400 prisoner, leaving just 1,000 survivors. By penetrating the Scottish defence lines Lambert had yet again broken the tactical stalemate, but this time Leslie's situation seemed far from desperate. He could counter the danger by using his interior lines of communication to move swiftly into Fife, where his much superior numbers would be expected to destroy Lambert's forces. In addition to leaving a strong garrison at Stirling, Leslie could also ensure that Cromwell would have to besiege it, thereby having no chance of crossing the Forth quickly enough to catch up with the Scottish army before it reached Lambert.

Following Lambert's success, Cromwell watched the movements in the Scottish camp through 'perspective glasses' as he had done at Dunbar and, once he was convinced Leslie was moving eastward with most of his army towards Inverkeithing, he began to return the English army to Edinburgh in order to ferry it across the Forth to meet Leslie in Fife. Cromwell remained in Edinburgh for a week, during which time the English seized the island fortress of Inchgarvie in the Firth of Forth and used every ship they could commandeer to ferry about 14,000 men across to Fife, leaving behind eight regiments in Edinburgh.

However, David Leslie, who had led Cromwell such a dance before Dunbar and during the armies' recent manoeuvrings before Stirling, had not lost his skills of deception. The prospect of meeting with Cromwell's main army in Fife was not one he relished and in any case from quite early in the year his king, Charles II, had favoured a move into England, where he anticipated Royalist supporters would join him in their thousands. When Leslie was sure Cromwell's army had left Bannnockburn for Edinburgh and Queensferry he halted his own army and began making preparations to move southward into England.

Whether Cromwell's removal of his smaller western garrisons was part of a deliberate ploy to lure the Scots into moving south or not, he had always been confident that if their army came out into the open he would be able to beat them again. Cromwell certainly anticipated Leslie making such an initiative, for he took pains to guard against it by placing General Thomas Harrison in charge of the English force at Carlisle. When Harrison came up to Edinburgh to garrison it in place of Overton, he had already been given instructions about making a southward march in the event of a Scottish invasion of England. Cromwell had also urged the English Council of State to put together another force at Chester.[8] At the least such forces could be sure to give the Scots 'some check' until Cromwell caught up with them.

Cromwell's confidence about the outcome was seen in a letter of 4 August to William Lenthall. This followed his taking of Perth which, by cutting off the Scottish army's provisions, gave it even less reason to remain in Scotland. Cromwell wrote the letter just prior to commencing his southward pursuit of Leslie and Charles II and in it

Towards Full Conquest   117

he explained to the Speaker how he believed that offering the Scots the option to invade England had indeed been the only way to move them into the open:

> If (Leslie) goes for England, being some few days march before us, it may trouble some men's thoughts; and may occasion some inconveniences. It may be supposed we might have kept the enemy from this, by interposing between him and England. Which truly I believe we might: *but how to remove him out of this place*, without doing what we have done, unless we had a commanding Army on both sides of the River of Forth is not clear to us; that this Enemy is heart-smitten by God; and whenever the Lord shall bring us up to them, we believe the Lord will make the desperateness of this counsel of theirs to appear, and the folly of it also.[9]

From then on the campaign would go forward as Cromwell had planned. Before moving in pursuit he left behind a garrison in Perth and also approximately 6,000 of his less experienced soldiers under General Monck with the task of capturing Stirling before moving on to conquer the rest of Scotland. John Buchan saw Cromwell's pursuit of the Scottish army in gladiatorial terms, where contingents under Harrison and Lambert, and formations of English militia under Fleetwood and Fairfax acted as the net, like that of the retiarius gladiator, with the main body of Puritan infantry under Cromwell's own command representing the trident.[10]

As in 1648, an alien Scottish army intending to march the length of England and seize London was moving to near-certain defeat. Yet in 1651, unlike the earlier Engagers' army, Charles II would find a considerable number of men – though still not enough – willing to join him in that dangerous, if not doomed, expedition. Soon after moving into England, desertions and casualties had reduced the Scottish army to 11,000 men, but at the time of its final battle at Worcester (which had become the Scots' objective once their path to London was no longer possible) it numbered 16,000, including 5,000 Englishmen who were moved to support a Stuart king.[11] Against this Cromwell had about 30,000 soldiers with a further 80,000 'rising in the distance to join him if need were'.[12] With such an overwhelming force Cromwell had no need to hurry: before fighting he could give his troops time to recover from their march and there was ample opportunity to assemble pontoon bridges with which to cross the rivers Severn and Teme guarding Worcester. He ordered in his main attack on 3 September, the anniversary of his success at Dunbar; the result was never in doubt, although the Royalists put up a determined resistance.

The details of a battle in which Cromwell and his hardened troops enjoyed a massive numerical superiority, and when over twice as many militia were positioned elsewhere in England, are not important here. With such superior numbers, far better artillery and purpose-built boats to cross Worcester's river screens, there was virtually no chance of Cromwell suffering a serious reverse. It was more a question of winning with the fewest casualties. Yet in spite of the largely expected result, Cromwell himself was never more energetic, 'riding up and down in the midst of the horse' and taking considerable personal risks during what he must have thought would be his last engagement. His opponent, Charles II, while inexperienced and with hopes that must surely have been low, also fought extremely well. As for their senior supporting commanders, David Leslie (whose role had been downgraded by the presence of his king) was for the most part a sad spectator, his cavalry committed in the first instance to the unlikely task of pursuing the defeated English and then not actively seeking another role elsewhere, while the incomparable Lambert was chiefly concerned with preparing the equipment and ensuring the crossings of the rivers Severn and Teme.

While the fighting had been severe on occasion, after three hours it was all over. Afterwards Cromwell acknowledged just 200 casualties, whereas the Scottish dead and wounded totalled about 2,000, with 10,000 others taken prisoner and just 4,000 making their escape from the beaten army – including, of course, Charles II. This time the prisoners faced no death march but all those below the rank of captain were destined for the plantations of Virginia and Bermuda, although in practice 1,000 were sent to contractors engaged in draining the Norfolk fens with orders that they be guarded closely.

Before Cromwell began his move southward in pursuit of Leslie he had given George Monck the task of taking Stirling and completing the conquest of Scotland. Cromwell had taken with him the most seasoned soldiers and the numbers under Monck's command were not large for such a task. Cromwell himself voiced doubts about their capacity to achieve it, for on 4 August his letter to Speaker Lenthall explaining his arrangements for pursuing Charles II ended with the guarded comment, 'I hope I have left a commanding force under Lieutenant-General Monck in Scotland.'[13] Scotland appeared fully capable of matching Monck's forces of about 6,000 soldiers, together with another 4,000 scattered in garrisons elsewhere in the country, with new levies from the traditional Scottish recruiting areas of the West and the Royalist north-east Highlands. However, with Leslie accompanying the king and his army, Charles II appointed the Earl of Crawford-Lindsay as commander in chief of his forces in Scotland. This was a political appointment on the king's part primarily designed to stop the Kirk party from taking advantage of his absence to recover its power. It was not a good choice in the military sense, for Crawford-Lindsay had been an unsuccessful commander for the Covenanters against Montrose, then an Engager leader who had only been allowed to participate in either military or political affairs by the very recent changes to the Act of Classes. Although he was now an ardent Royalist, after such a chequered career and understandably being highly unpopular with the Kirk party, he was by no means the best man to bring together the different military factions needed to defend their Scottish heartland. His task was made more difficult, as from the outset Monck adopted a most confident and aggressive stance, setting about his task with a rapidity that would have surprised Cromwell himself. He moved first against Stirling, calling upon the fortress to surrender. Despite its formidable defences the town quickly submitted, although most of its troops moved into the castle. Monck, who had by now become expert in the use of artillery, then began to bombard the castle and as early as 14 August the plunging fire from his mortars had forced its garrison to surrender.

While conducting the siege Monck sent Colonel Okey with 1,400 mounted troops to help subdue the West, which task he very largely accomplished. Monck next marched eastward and moved up the Fife coast towards Dundee. At the same time he received an unexpected but massive bonus, when cavalry under Colonel Alured, which had been sent ahead, surprised and scattered a force of some 5,000 Scots at Alyth, about fifteen miles from Dundee, before going on to capture most of the current Scottish political and military leaders, including Crawford-Lindsay and Leven, together with many representatives from the Scottish Committee of Estates and the commission of its Assembly.

On 1 September Monck commenced his assault on Dundee, whose population had been swelled by refugees from Scotland's other cities. He offered its garrison the opportunity to surrender but it refused, having mistakenly heard news of a Scottish victory at Worcester. After breaking in, Monck granted his soldiers twenty-four hours' plunder, during which 800 people were killed and valuables to a value of £200,000 sterling were seized, with 'individual soldiers enriched to the tune of 500 pounds each'.[14] The slaughter at Dundee led other towns, like Montrose and Aberdeen, to submit quickly, for by this time accounts from soldiers who had managed to escape left no doubt about the defeat of their main army at Worcester.

Cromwell's last military campaign against Scotland had run a full and successful course after its turning point at Dunbar the previous year. However unexpected, Cromwell's success there gave him the chance to regain the initiative and led directly to his victory at Worcester and to Monck's completion of the conquest of Scotland. By early September the country was utterly crushed: it had no army left, most of its ruling elite were in captivity, its king was a fugitive and its main towns were occupied by English troops. Scotland had paid a fearful price for its involvement in the Civil Wars, particularly during the years 1648–51 when fighting directly against Cromwell. The 3,000 casualties and 10,000 prisoners taken by him and Lambert in 1648 were augmented by a further 5,000 killed and 20,000 prisoners from the Battles of Dunbar and Worcester. With Scotland's population at this time standing at less than a million, of whom about 200,000 were male adults, the human cost of fighting their more populous and more powerful neighbour had proved terribly high, quite apart from the collateral damage suffered by their country being fought over and 'scorched'. Yet even these figures were dwarfed by the sufferings of Ireland over the same period, where at Cromwell's hands the loss of life was fourfold that of Scotland's.[15]

The sombre fact for Scotland was that from the thirteenth century onwards, when the country was fighting for its independence against Edward I, until its encounters with the regicide Cromwell four centuries later, Scottish armies – despite their formidable soldiers – required exceptional and above all united leadership to beat the generally better-resourced and often technically superior English forces. This happened on two notable occasions, under William Wallace and Robert Bruce. In 1297 at Stirling Bridge Wallace was able to catch and destroy a portion of a much superior English army as it moved to attack him across Stirling's long and narrow river bridge, a victory that delayed Edward I's subjection of Scotland and played a major part in Robert Bruce taking up the cause of Scotland's independence. Seventeen years later at Bannockburn Robert Bruce's peerless generalship outmatched his opposing monarch, Edward II, and enabled him to confine the English in a deadly pocket enclosed by two watercourses, where only a fraction of their assembled army was in any position to fight. As a result of Bruce's victory and his subsequent military superiority, Scotland was able to regain its independence fourteen years later.

The third instance of a Scottish battlefield success standing a good chance of changing the contemporary military balance between the two warring countries should by all expectations have been at Dunbar on 3 September 1650. After the English had been outwitted, outmanoeuvred and reduced to half their opponent's numbers (with many of the remaining soldiers by no means fit) they should have been defeated. Following a heavy defeat, with Cromwell possibly killed or captured, the future of the Commonwealth would at best have been uncertain. In his absence Royalist morale would have risen dramatically and the Royalist uprisings so effectively put down by the Puritan authorities during the year after the battle would, in all probability, have succeeded.

That the English were, in reality, not beaten at Dunbar but, like Wallace and Bruce, succeeded in preventing their opponents from deploying their superior military resources, owed something to a degree of Scottish over-confidence and to that other dire thread running throughout Scottish military history, the weakness of divided leadership (emanating this time from religious differences) which had so often betrayed their fighting men.

Even so, it was not so much Scottish failures at Dunbar as outstanding leadership on the part of Oliver Cromwell and his remarkable subordinates, who perceived a most unlikely opportunity to catch their opponents off balance, and went on to seize it brilliantly. Such a gamble was made feasible by the doughty fighting men of Cromwell's own creation, his New Model Army who, through their loyalty to their commander in chief, their pride in their soldiering, close identification with their particular units and acceptance of the high levels of discipline required by their commander, were to set the standards for the future British army recruited from all its home countries.

Nonetheless, throughout Cromwell's remarkable military career, marked by almost unbroken successes, none of his battlefield victories was more surprising, nor ultimately more conclusive, than that achieved by his veteran Calvinist sectaries, ailing and bedraggled as they were, at Dunbar on 3 September 1650.

The Present Battlefield

Intending visitors should be in possession of an Ordnance Survey Explorer map number 351, scale 1:25,000 ($2^1/_2$ inches to the mile), covering Dunbar and North Berwick, and including Musselburgh and Haddington. A pair of binoculars would also be advantageous. The directions that follow assume you have the use of a car and that you are prepared to walk for reasonable distances both along tracks and over rough grassland.

Surrounding Area

Before considering the main battle, you can use your map to track the journey made by Cromwell during his initial invasion from Cockburnspath via Dunbar to Musselburgh or, for that matter, follow his retreat from Musselburgh via Haddington back to Dunbar. You might even wish to pay a visit to the remarkable Tantallon Castle (GR 597 851) near North Berwick (under the care of Scottish Heritage), which was severely damaged by George Monck before he persuaded its governor, Alexander Seaton, to surrender to him on 21 February 1651.

The Battle of Dunbar

Although the centre-point of the battlefield (denoted by the usual crossed swords symbol) is some 250 metres south-east of Dunbar, close to the present A1 trunk road, it is not accessible to visitors and the stone commemorating the battle has been repositioned nearby. (More of this later.)

   Like many other sites in Britain, the one commemorating the battle at Dunbar on 3 September 1650 is not well presented. It has no viewscape, lacks explanatory boards for visitors to follow a trail round the field, and there is no visitor centre. (Remarkably, there are even fewer clues to Dunbar's earlier battle during 1296, which took place in the Spott valley some 2,000 metres away.)

   As well as the lack of explanatory instructions, after an interval of more than 350 years significant developments have occurred to the site. It is presently crossed by a major trunk road, the A1, and the original road over the battlefield has partially disappeared. Improvements made to the A1 have caused the battle's memorial stone to be removed to its present location along the A1087 at GR 698 769, while since the mid-nineteenth century the battlefield has also been intersected by the East Coast main railway line running from Berwick to Edinburgh.

Yet, without question, the development most affecting the battle site has been the building of a large cement works adjoining it, which has led to extensive quarrying on the field itself. As a result the conformation of the ground across which the main cavalry encounters took place has been changed both by quarrying and the spread of spoil. In spite of this, by careful comparison with the adjoining land it is still possible to envisage this area as it was in 1650, while (unlike many other battle sites) most of the remaining area and its environs have remained unchanged. The problems for today's battlefield enthusiasts who wish to visit Dunbar come not so much from geophysical changes as from inaccessibility. For the most part the battle was fought over land which is extensively farmed (and fenced), with Broxmouth House part of a private estate.

By now some readers could well be wondering whether a visit to the field is worth the trouble. The answer is unquestionably yes. Although such problems are daunting and make a visitor cover far more ground than he might have anticipated, by using a map, together with the battle diagrams in this book, it is still possible to deduce what probably happened on that fateful morning of 3 September 1650, while at the same time enjoying the truly spectacular countryside of the area.

* * * *

You are recommended to begin in Dunbar at the parish church (GR 682 786), which stands on a small promontory to the south of the old town, beside the A1087 leading to the battlefield. (For parking there is a lay-by to its front.) The parish church, founded 1176, is a large and distinctive building with an extensive churchyard and it was here that Cromwell first placed his artillery train after his retreat from Haddington. From the churchyard you can see across to Doon Hill (GR 685 757) lying almost due south, which the Scottish army had already occupied, together with the flat ground below it through which the Brox Burn runs. To your left are the extensive trees within the walled Broxmouth estate. When you have taken your bearings you can drive south along the A1087, noting on your right Newtonlees Farm, the second location of the English artillery, before you come to where your road crosses the Brox Burn at GR 694 772. It was from here that Lambert commenced his attack upon the Scottish cavalry. Moving on, to your left is the wall of the Broxmouth estate and on the right an unmetalled road leading to Brand's Mill, where the English infantry under George Monck began their assault. After a further 700 metres you will see on your left-hand side the monument commemorating the battle.

Having followed the main English movements up to the time Lambert and Monck launched their attacks across the burn, it is suggested you move on to Doon Hill, from where you can look at the battlefield from the Scottish perspective.

James Smer
Andrew Kenner
Jo Camel
John Steward
Allen Osborn
John Wilson
Walter Wanhop
Patrick Warburton
William Ingles
Alexander Gourdon
Samuel Gourdon
Lancaster Harkenson
Robert Rankin
Cha Colemine
John Rawson
Andrew Guiler

Geo Totterson
Thomas Hutchen
John Emnes
John Skew
John Hunter
John Markdoughal
Andrew Drummon
George Moale
Francis Scot
Alexander Kiff
John Markdoughil
George Lesley
William Livery
John Denant
William Elliot

George Windram, cornet
Thomas Collerwood, cornet
Patrick Lindsey, cornet
Captain William Brisbon, of horse
William Cunningham, cornet
James Maxwel, cornet
James Denham, cornet
James Bruse, lieutenant of horse
John Magel, cornet

Walter Steward, cornet
John Hay, cornet
William Danrimple, captain of foot
Captain Charles Kirkpatrick
Captain Nicholas Lawson
Jas Magavite, cornet
John Brown, cornet
Alex Michel, cornet

Quartermasters of Horse
Thomas Richinson

William Fabus

Ensigns of Foot
Kilpatrick
Walter MacDoghal
William Sanckle
Gorge Jack
Hartley Gud
William Carnetuss
Thomas Wallis
Andrew Myan
James Bennet
John Linsey
Andrew Hanna

Thomas Pringle
Robert Hamilton
James Delap
John Gunny
John Edwards
Colin Camel
Heatly
Robert Ray
Gilbert Hurral
James Musket
William Simple

Robert Ogleby
Robert Williamson
William Lesley
Ersbield Shields
Robert Habern
William Scot
James Edmaston
Robert Lawson
James Newen
Andrew Bathick
George Elphenson
John Hindise
Henry Whittle
Andrew Donnalson
David Kenede
John Camel
Dunkin Kemel
Cornelius Engles
Patrick Calion
William Mawood
Henry Kertebrik
Alex Chalmers
George Crime
James Rede
John Somervil
John Abenille
John Clark
Alexander Breme
William Chapman
John Muckin
Alexander Spence
John Mark
Thomas Thompson
John Dixon
John Smith
Alexander Johnson
William Egger
David Grant
George Guyle
John Wallis
John Kemen
Thomas Anderson
James Brewse

William Mamblan
James Carmibil
William Watsin
William Anderson
James Dunbarre
James Calderwood
Hugh Rey
Thomas Bayde
David Beed
Robert Craw
George Calley
James Rutherford
Walter Scot
Walter Steward
Robert Henne
James Facquer
James Marmath
Hentry Ackman
John Weare
John Brown-Lee
David Bisket
George Hinderson
John Blacketter
Alexander Michel
Alexander Baily
Robert Wallwood
John Watson
William Greere
John Crawford
William Wilson
John Dunbar
Samuel Gurdon
John Munins
John Cunningham
William Staolin
Alexander Guthery
John Hunter
Adam Luckey
Andrew Mayrey
Robert Macktellon
Robert Gerne
John Mackews
James Brotherston

William Gentry
Edward Sincler
Andrew Brede

Robert Hunter
John Gray

Sergeants
Henry Muckerry
Alexander Sibbet
Gilbert Gray
James Ellis
Collin Gardner
John Axenhead
John Hogg
William Watson

John Mackwel
James Lyel
James Coddel
John Morris
Adam Kerk

Captain Robert Rutherford of foot
Captain John Car of foot

The whole number of officers and private soldiers taken, 10,000
4,000 slain
32 pieces of ordnance of all sorts
200 colours, horse and foot
All their arms, tents, bag and baggage.

Appendix B

The Lord General's Proclamation concerning the wounded men left on the field

Forasmuch as I understand there are several soldiers of the enemy army yet abiding in the field, who, by reason of their wounds, could not march from thence: these are therefore to give notice to the inhabitants of this nation, that they may and have free liberty to repair to the field aforesaid, and with their carts, or any other peaceable way, to carry the said soldiers to such places as they shall think fit; provided they meddle not or take away any of the arms there; and all officers and soldiers are to take notice that the same is permitted. Given under my hand at Dunbar.

Sept 4 1650   O. Cromwell

                         To be proclaimed by beat of drum

('Several proceedings in Parliament, No. 50, 5–12 September 1650: Thomas Carlyle, *Oliver Cromwell's Letters and Speeches*, 3 vols (London, 1846), vol. 2, pp. 209–10.)

Appendix C

The Composition of the English Army

Cavalry

First Cavalry Brigade
Brigade Commander, Major General John Lambert

Regiment of General Charles Fleetwood
Regiment of Major General John Lambert
Regiment of Colonel Edward Whalley

Second Cavalry Brigade
Brigade Commander, Colonel Robert Lilburne

Regiment of Colonel Robert Lilburne
Regiment of Colonel Francis Hacker
Regiment of Colonel Philip Twisleton

Lord General's Cavalry Regiment
Commander, Captain Packer

Dragoons (Six Companies)
Commander, Colonel John Okey

Infantry

First Infantry Brigade
Brigade Commander, Colonel George Monck

Regiment of Colonel George Monck
Regiment of Colonel John Malverer
Regiment of Colonel George Fenwick

Second Infantry Brigade
Brigade Commander, Colonel Thomas Pride

Regiment of Colonel Thomas Pride
Regiment of The Lord General (Cromwell)
Regiment of Major General John Lambert

Third Infantry Brigade
Brigade Commander, Colonel Robert Overton

Regiment of Colonel Alban Coxe
Regiment of Colonel William Daniel
Regiment of Colonel Charles Fairfax

The Artillery Train of 690 all ranks had eight to ten siege guns and twelve field pieces.

The army's full establishment at the time it crossed the border was 16,354 all ranks, plus 690 with the artillery train, but at the Battle of Dunbar Cromwell maintained it was down to between 11,500 and 12,000 men.

Appendix D
The Composition of the Scottish Army

The Scottish Army's organization is less clear cut. A singular way of inquiring into the Scottish Army at Dunbar was made by interviewing Scottish prisoners of war, the results of which are to be found in the *Harleian Manuscript*, No. 6844, fo. 123. Much the most thorough research so far in this arcane area has been conducted by Edward Furgol in his *A Regimental History of the Covenanting Armies 1639–1651* (Edinburgh, 1990).

Cavalry Formations
The *Harleian Manuscript* put the Scottish horse regiments at eighteen. These totalled about 7,000 men and had widely differing complements. Although Major General Sir Robert Montgomerie was in command of their first line and Colonel Archibald Strachan of the second, it did not name the cavalry brigade commanders and the following suggestions by the present author are necessarily tentative.

Cavalry

First Cavalry Brigade
Brigade Commander, Major General Sir John Browne

Second Cavalry Brigade
Brigade Commander, Colonel Archibald Strachan

Third Cavalry Brigade
Brigade Commander, Colonel William Stewart

Fourth Cavalry Brigade
Brigade Commander, Major General Sir Robert Montgomerie

Fifth Cavalry Brigade
Brigade Commander, Lieutenant General David Leslie

Sixth Cavalry Brigade
Brigade Commander, Earl of Leven

Dragoons
The three regiments of dragoons with the Scottish army were those of:
Sir John Douglas of Mouswall
William Menzies
Colonel John of Kirkcudbright.

Infantry
The Scottish infantry brigade commanders are identified in the *Harleian Manuscript* and their regimental commanders follow the proposals made by Stuart Reid based on Edward Furgol's researches.

First Infantry Brigade
Brigade Commander, Lieutenant General Sir James Lumsden

Regiment of Sir James Lumsden
Regiment of the General of the Artillery
Regiment of Sir William Douglas of Kirkness

Second Infantry Brigade
Brigade Commander, Major General Sir James Holborn

Regiment of Major General Sir James Holborn
Regiment of Sir George Buchannan of Buchannan
Regiment (from Edinburgh) of Colonel Alexander Stewart

Third Infantry Brigade
Brigade Commander, Major General Colin Pitscottie

Regiment of Major General Colin Pitscottie
Regiment of Sir David Home of Wedderburn
Regiment of Colonel John Lindsay of Edzell

Fourth Infantry Brigade
Brigade Commander, Colonel Sir James Campbell of Lawers

Regiment of Sir James Campbell of Lawers
Regiment of Sir George Preston of Valleyfield
Regiment of Sir John Haldane of Gleneagles

Fifth Infantry Brigade
Brigade Commander, Colonel John Innes

Regiment of Colonel John Innes
Regiment of Colonel John Forbes
Regiment of Master of Lovat

English sources put the total Scottish infantry strength at about 16,000.

The Artillery Train of some 400 all ranks had thirty-two pieces of ordnance, including light guns.

Appendix E
Matchlock Muskets

The problems posed by such muskets – so apparent at Dunbar – were subsequently highlighted in the Earl of Orrery's *Treatise on the Art of War* published in 1677.

With the Fire-lock you have only to cock, and you are prepared to shoot; but with your match-lock you have several motions, the least of which is as long a performing, as but that one of the other, and often times much more hazardous; besides, if you fire not the match-lock musket as soon as you have blown your match (which often, especially in hedge fights and in sieges, you cannot do), you must a second time blow your match, or the ashes it gathers hinders it from firing.

Secondly, the match is very dangerous, either where bandeleers are used, or where soldiers run hastily in fight to the budge-barrel, to refill their bandeleers; I have often seen sad instances thereof.

Thirdly, marching in the nights to avoid an enemy, or to surprize one, or to assault a fortress, the matches often discover you, and inform the enemy where you are, whereby you suffer much, and he obtains much.

Fourthly, in wet weather, the pan of the musket being made wide open for a while, the rain often deads the powder, and the match too; and in windy weather, blows away the powder, ere the match can touch the pan: nay, often in very high winds, I have seen the sparks blown from the match, fire the musket ere the soldier meant it; and either thereby lose his shot, or wound or kill someone before him. Whereas in the fire-lock, the motion is so sudden, that what makes the cock fall on the hammer, strikes the fire, and opens the pan at once.

Lastly, to omit many other reasons, the quantity of match used in an army, does much add to the baggage, and being of a very dry quality, naturally draws the moisture of the air, which makes it relax, and consequently less fit, though carried in close wagons: and without being dried in ovens, is but of half the use which otherwise it would be of: and which is full as bad the skeans you give the corporals, and the links you give the private soldiers (of which near an enemy, or on the ordinary guard duty, they must never be unfurnished), if they lodge in huts or tents; or if they keep guard in the open field (as most often it happens) all the match for instant service is too often rendered uncertain or useless; nothing of all which can be said of the flint, but much of it to the contrary.

And then the soldiers generally wearing their links of match near the bottom of the belt, on which their bandeleers are fastened, in wet weather generally spoil the match they have, and if they are to fight on a sudden, and in the rain, you lose the use of your small shot which is sometimes of irreparable prejudice.

(Quoted in Francis Grose, *Military Antiquities respecting a History of the English Army, from the Conquest to the Present Time* (London, 1801), vol. 2, pp. 129–30.)

Notes

Chapter 1: England and Scotland 1638–1647

1. During 1562 the Thirty-Nine Articles were agreed upon in London by the archbishops, bishops and the whole clergy of the Provinces of Canterbury and York.
2. Robert Baillie, *The Letters and Journals of Robert Baillie*, ed. D. Laing, 3 vols (Edinburgh, Bannatyne Club, 1841–2), vol. 2, p. 361.
3. *The Basilikon Doron of King James VI*, ed. James Craigie (Scottish Texts Society, 1944), p. 1.
4. Ibid., p. 7.
5. Sir Antony Weldon, *The Court and Character of King James* (London, 1650), p. 177.
6. Gordon Donaldson, *Scotland: James V to James VII* (Edinburgh, 1990), p. 300.
7. Baillie, *Letters and Journals*, vol. 2, p. 12.
8. Ibid., vol. 1, p. 111.
9. *Calendar of State Papers Domestic* (1639), p. 243.
10. John Rushworth, *Historical Collections of Private Passages of State* (London, 1659–1701), vol. 2, pp. 1131–63.
11. Mark Nobel, *Memoirs of the Protectorate House of Cromwell* (Edinburgh, 1787), vol. 1, p. 268.
12. W C Abbott, *Writings and Speeches of Oliver Cromwell*, 4 vols (Cambridge, MA, 1937–47), vol. 1, p. 314.
13. Trevor Royle, *Civil War: The Wars of the Three Kingdoms, 1638–1660* (London, 2004), pp. 278–9.

Chapter 2: Auld Enemies Again 1648–1650

1. Baillie, *Letters and Journals*, vol. 3, p. 15.
2. Bishop Gilbert Burnet, *Memoirs of the Lives and Actions of James and William, Dukes of Hamilton and Castlehead* (London, 1677), p. 432.

3. The name came from the Scottish word whig, meaning to spur a horse.
4. Abbott, *Writings and Speeches of Oliver Cromwell*, vol. 1, p. 639.
5. Royle, *Civil War*, p. 487.
6. Raymond Campbell Paterson, *A Land Afflicted: Scotland and the Covenanter Wars 1638–1690* (Edinburgh, 1998), p. 172.
7. Tom Reilly's revisionist account published in 1999, which attempts to exculpate Cromwell from 'wholesale and indiscriminate slaughter', is entitled *Cromwell: An Honourable Enemy*.
8. Frank Kitson, *Old Ironsides: The Military Biography of Oliver Cromwell* (London, 2004), p. 169.
9. John Buchan, *Oliver Cromwell* (London, 1934), p. 338.
10. Christopher Hill, *God's Englishman: Oliver Cromwell and the English Revolution* (London, 1970), pp. 108–12.
11. Kitson, *Old Ironsides*, p. 175.
12. Buchan, *Oliver Cromwell*, p. 347.
13. Thomas Carlyle, *Oliver Cromwell's Letters and Speeches*, 3 vols (London, 1846), vol. 1, Letter CIX, p. 100.
14. John D. Grainger, *Cromwell Against the Scots: The Last Anglo-Scottish War, 1650–1652* (East Linton, 1997), p. 10.
15. Ibid., p. 12.
16. James Scott Wheeler, *The Irish and British Wars 1637–1654: Triumph, Tragedy, and Failure* (London, 2002), p. 220.

Chapter 3: The English Army and its Commanders

1. The Northern Parliamentary Army commanded by Lord Fairfax operated mainly in Yorkshire.
2. C H Firth, *The Battle of Dunbar* (Transactions of the Royal Historical Society, New Series 14, 1899), p. 25.
3. Stuart Reid, *Dunbar 1650* (Oxford, 2004), p. 29.
4. C H Firth, *Cromwell's Army: A History of the English Soldier during the Civil Wars, the Commonwealth and the Protectorate* (London, 1962), p. 322.
5. C E Lucas Phillips, *Cromwell's Captains* (London and Toronto, 1938), p. 293.
6. Firth, *Cromwell's Army*, p. 110.
7. Ibid., p. 120.
8. Francis Grose, *Military Antiquities respecting a History of the English Army, from the Conquest to the Present Time* (London, 1801), vol. 2, p. 125.
9. Sir Thomas Kellie, *Pallas Armata* (Edinburgh, 1627), p. 110.
10. Grose, *Military Antiquities*, vol. 2, p. 339.
11. John Hodgson, *Memoirs of Captain John Hodgson* (Edinburgh, 1806), p. 260.
12. A W Wilson, *The Story of the Gun* (Woolwich, Royal Artillery Institution, 1944), p. 21.
13. Captain Harry Hexham, *Principalls of the Art Militaire* (Delf, 1642), part 3, pp. 13–15.

14. Alan Turton and Stuart Peachey, *An Introduction to the Armies of the First English Civil War 1642–1646* (Bristol, 1993), p. 12.

15. John Norris, *Artillery: A History* (Stroud, 2000), p. 86.

16. Carlyle, *Cromwell's Letters and Speeches*, vol. 2, Letter XCIX, p. 64.

17. Buchan, *Oliver Cromwell*, p. 522.

18. Antonia Fraser, *Cromwell, Our Chief of Men* (London, 1973), p. 704.

19. Charles Firth, *Oliver Cromwell and the Rule of the Puritans in England* (London, 1923), p. 467.

20. Unfortunately most of these appear to have been burnt in 1847 'in order to prevent family feuds from arising': T S Baldock, *Cromwell as a Soldier* (1899), pp. 516–17.

21. Firth, *Oliver Cromwell*, pp. 468–9.

22. D L Hobman, *Cromwell's Master Spy: A Study of John Thurloe* (London, 1961), p. 17.

23. Alan Marshall, *Oliver Cromwell, Soldier* (London, 2004), p. 273.

24. Bulstrode Whitelocke, *Memorials of the English Affairs from the Beginning of the Reign of Charles I to King Charles II's Happy Restoration* (London, 1722), vol. 1, p. 256.

25. *Dictionary of National Biography*, vol. 7 (1908), p. 262.

26. Phillips, *Cromwell's Captains*, p. 343.

27. Ibid., p. 279.

28. Ibid., p. 261.

29. *Dictionary of National Biography*, vol. 11 (1909), p. 452.

30. Fraser, *Cromwell, Our Chief of Men*, p. 203.

31. Phillips, *Cromwell's Captains*, p. 292.

32. Hodgson, *Memoirs*, p. 145.

33. *Mercurius Politicus*, 24–31 July 1650.

34. Carlyle, *Cromwell's Letters and Speeches*, vol. 2, Letter CLXI, p. 319.

35. Thomas Skinner, *The Life of General Monck, Duke of Albemarle* (London, 1724), p. xix.

36. Thomas Gumble, *The Life of General Monck, Duke of Albemarle* (London, 1671), pp. 35–8; Carlyle, *Cromwell's Letters and Speeches*, vol. 2, Letter CXXVII, 4 September 1650, p. 213.

37. *Dictionary of National Biography*, vol. 13 (1909), p. 599.

38. Ibid., p. 604.

39. Samuel Pepys, *Diary*, 23 October 1667.

Chapter 4: The Scottish Army and its Commanders

1. *Acts of the Parliaments of Scotland*, vol. 6, Part 2, p. 597.

2. In all, this army had numbered 6,000 infantry, 11,200 horse and 200 dragoons.

3. *Acts of the Parliaments of Scotland*, vol. 6, Part 2, p. 597.

4. Edward M Furgol, *A Regimental History of the Covenanting Armies 1639–1651* (Edinburgh, 1990), p. 366.

5. Ibid., p. 362.
6. *Acts of the Parliaments of Scotland*, vol. 6, Part 2, p. 586; Grainger, *Cromwell Against the Scots*, p. 29.
7. Sir Edward Walker, *Historical Discourses* (London, 1705), p. 163.
8. Carlyle, *Cromwell's Letters and Speeches*, vol. 2, Letter CXXII, p. 184.
9. Reid, *Dunbar 1650*, pp. 67, 68.
10. Hodgson, *Memoirs*, p. 277.
11. Peter Reese, *Bannockburn: Scotland's Greatest Victory* (Edinburgh, 2003), pp. 162, 163.
12. Firth, *Cromwell's Army*, pp. 126–7.
13. Furgol, *A Regimental History of the Covenanting Armies*, p. 297.
14. Firth, *Cromwell's Army*, p. 149.
15. *Mercurius Politicus*, 12–19 September 1650.
16. David Stevenson and David Caldwell, 'Leather guns and other light artillery in mid-17th century Scotland', *Proceedings of the Society of Antiquarians for Scotland*, 108 (1976–7), p. 306.
17. An amazing twenty-three of Wemyss's cannon survive today and among them a main group of nineteen 'probably constitute the closest approximation to a complete light artillery train of the 17th century to survive anywhere in Britain' (Stevenson and Caldwell, 'Leather guns and other light artillery', p. 308).
18. James Burns, *Memoirs by James Burns 1644–1661* (Edinburgh, 1832), p. 16; C H Firth, 'Site of Battle of Dunbar', *Transactions of the Royal Historical Society* (1899), p. 31.
19. Peter Reese, *The Scottish Commander: Scotland's Greatest Military Leaders from Wallace to World War II* (Edinburgh, 1999), p. 111.
20. *Acts of the Parliaments of Scotland*, vol. 6, Part 2, p. 598.
21. Samuel R Gardiner, *History of the Great Civil War 1642–1649*, 4 vols (London, 1898), vol. 2, p. 2.
22. Ibid., p. 356.
23. William Anderson, *The Scottish Nation: or, The Surnames, Families, Literature, Honours, and Biographical History of the People of Scotland*, 3 vols (Edinburgh, 1862), vol. 3, p. 383.
24. *Acts of the Parliaments of Scotland*, vol. 6, Part 2, p. 167.
25. Edward J Cowan, *Montrose: For Covenant and King* (London, 1977), pp. 177, 292.
26. Ronald Williams, *Montrose: Cavalier in Mourning* (London, 1975), p. 53.
27. Letter of A Guinan dated 10 August 2005 to the author.
28. Charles Sanford Terry, *The Life and Campaigns of Alexander Leslie, First Earl of Leven* (London, 1899), p. 1.
29. Sir William Fraser, *The Melvilles, Earls of Melville and the Leslies, Earls of Leven* (Edinburgh, 1890), vol. 3, p. 385.
30. Baillie, *Letters and Journals*, vol. 1, p. 11.
31. Terry, *Life and Campaigns of Alexander Leslie*, p. 155.

32. Carlyle, *Cromwell's Letters and Speeches*, vol. 1, p. 415, explanatory notes following Letter LXXI.
33. Reese, *The Scottish Commander*, pp. 106–9.
34. W Fraser, *Memorials of the Montgomeries, Earls of Eglinton*, 2 vols (Edinburgh, 1859), vol. 1, p. 3.
35. Carlyle, *Cromwell's Letters and Speeches*, vol. 1, Letter LXXI, pp. 413–14.
36. Ibid., vol. 2, Letter CXXII, p. 183.
37. *Dictionary of National Biography* (1909), vol. 12, p. 277.
38. *Oxford Dictionary of National Biography* (Oxford, 2004), vol. 34, p. 760.
39. Ibid., vol. 52, p. 988.
40. Ibid.

Chapter 5: Probing the Scottish Defences

1. Baillie, *Letters and Journals*, vol. 3, p. 68.
2. Royle, *Civil War*, p. 543.
3. Hodgson, *Memoirs*, p. 130.
4. Kitson, *Old Ironsides*, p. 189.
5. W S Douglas, *Cromwell's Scotch Campaigns 1650–51* (London, 1898), p. 38n.
6. *Calendar of State Papers Domestic* (1650), pp. 242–7.
7. Royle, *Civil War*, p. 575.
8. Hodgson, *Memoirs*, p. 131.
9. Whitelocke, *Memorials of the English Affairs*, p. 223.
10. Hodgson, *Memoirs*, p. 129.
11. Carlyle, *Cromwell's Letters and Speeches*, vol. 2, p. 181.
12. Ibid, p. 180.
13. Grainger, *Cromwell Against the Scots*, p. 37.
14. Carlyle, *Cromwell's Letters and Speeches*, vol. 2, p. 182.
15. James Miller, *The Lamp of Lothian, or the History of Haddington* (Edinburgh, 1844), p. 216.
16. C H Firth and G Davies, *The Regimental History of Cromwell's Army*, 2 vols (Oxford, 1940), vol. 1, pp. 87–8.
17. Carlyle, *Cromwell's Letters and Speeches*, vol. 2, p. 183.
18. Ibid., p. 184.
19. Ibid., p. 188.
20. Hodgson, *Memoirs*, p. 138.
21. *Mercurius Politicus*, 12–19 September 1650.
22. Douglas, *Cromwell's Scotch Campaigns*, p. 73.
23. *Mercurius Politicus*, No. 13, p. 206.
24. J Nicoll, *A Diary of Public Transactions and other Occurrences, chiefly in Scotland, from January 1650 to June 1667* (Edinburgh, Bannatyne Club, 1836), p. 25.
25. *Fullerton's Imperial Gazetteer of Scotland*, ed. Rev. Marius Wilson (Edinburgh, 1853), vol. 1, p. 814.
26. Ibid.

27. Carlyle, *Cromwell's Letters and Speeches*, vol. 2, Letter CXXV, p. 196.
28. Letter of 14 July 2005 from A Guinan to the author.
29. Marshall, *Oliver Cromwell*, p. 244.
30. Hodgson, *Memoirs*, p. 143.
31. Carlyle, *Cromwell's Letters and Speeches*, vol. 2, p. 198.
32. Douglas, *Cromwell's Scotch Campaigns*, p. 93.

Chapter 6: Back to Dunbar
1. Carlyle, *Cromwell's Letters and Speeches*, vol. 2, Letter CXXVII, p. 212.
2. *Mercurius Politicus*, 12–19 September 1650.
3. Kitson, *Old Ironsides*, p. 195.
4. Carlyle, *Cromwell's Letters and Speeches*, vol. 2, p. 212.
5. Ibid., p. 213.
6. Walker, *Historical Discourses*, p. 623.
7. Douglas, *Cromwell's Scotch Campaigns*, p. 94. Douglas cites the contemporary English observer, Sir Edward Walker, among others, for his conviction that it was the ministers who dissuaded Leslie from attacking.
8. Carlyle, *Cromwell's Letters and Speeches*, vol. 2, p. 198.
9. R J M Pugh, *Swords, Loaves and Fishes: A History of Dunbar from Earliest Times to the Present* (Balerno, 2003), p. 176.
10. Nicoll, *A Diary of Public Transactions*, p. 24.
11. Douglas, *Cromwell's Scotch Campaigns*, p. 92.
12. Thomas Carte, *A Collection of Original Letters and Papers concerning the Affairs of England from the Year 1641 to 1660*, 2 vols (London, 1739), vol. 1, p. 381.
13. Ibid.
14. Ibid.
15. Carlyle, *Cromwell's Letters and Speeches*, vol. 2, Letter CXXVI, p. 201.
16. Ibid., p. 203.
17. Douglas, *Cromwell's Scotch Campaigns*, pp. 95–105.
18. Carlyle, *Cromwell's Letters and Speeches*, vol. 2, Letter CXXIX, p. 223.
19. *House of Commons Journals*, vol. 6, p. 464.
20. Bishop Gilbert Burnet, *History of His Own Times* (London, 1724–34), vol. 1, p. 96.
21. Ibid.
22. Ibid., p. 97.

Chapter 7: Delivering Them into Our Hands
1. The names Spott, Brox and Brock have been used of the burn that runs from Spott village. The name Spott is here used of the burn where it runs through the ravine close to the village, and Brox where it reaches the vicinity of Broxburn hamlet and Broxmouth House.
2. Carlyle, *Cromwell's Letters and Speeches*, vol. 2, Letter CXXVII, p. 214.
3. Baldock, *Cromwell as a Soldier*, p. 455.

4. Carlyle, *Cromwell's Letters and Speeches*, vol. 2, p. 214.

5. The mill has been 'gentrified', together with the outbuildings, and is no longer used for its original purpose.

6. Thomas Carte, *Original Letters and Papers*, vol. 1, p. 382.

7. Samuel R Gardiner, *History of the Commonwealth and Protectorate 1649–1656*, 4 vols (London, 1903), vol. 1, p. 322.

8. Douglas, *Cromwell's Scotch Campaigns*, p. 107.

9. Gardiner, *History of the Commonwealth and Protectorate*, vol. 1, p. 290.

10. Carlyle, *Cromwell's Letters and Speeches*, vol. 2, p. 206.

11. 'A True Relation of Some Affairs', in Hodgson, *Memoirs*, p. 323.

12. Gardiner, *History of the Commonwealth and Protectorate*, vol. 1, p. 290.

13. Reid, *Dunbar 1650*, p. 62.

14. Hodgson, *Memoirs*, pp. 145–6.

15. Ibid., p. 146.

16. John Aubrey, *Miscellanies upon Various Subjects*, 5th edn (London, 1890), p. 143; Marshall, *Oliver Cromwell*, p. 248.

17. Carlyle, *Cromwell's Letters and Speeches*, vol. 2, p. 205.

Chapter 8: Face to Face

1. Carte, *Original Letters and Papers*, vol. 1, p. 383.

2. James Somerville, *Memorie of the Somervilles: being a History of the Baronial House of Somerville*, ed. Sir W. Scott, 2 vols (Edinburgh, 1815), vol. 2, p. 421; Firth, 'Site of Battle of Dunbar', pp. 39–40.

3. Gardiner, *History of the Commonwealth and Protectorate*, vol. 1, p. 325.

4. P Hume Brown, *History of Scotland to the Present Time*, 3 vols (Cambridge, 1911), vol. 2, p. 359; Nicoll, *A Diary of Public Transactions*, p. 28.

5. Chris Henry, *English Civil War Artillery 1642–51* (Oxford, 2005), p. 37.

6. *Mercurius Politicus*, 12–19 September 1650.

7. Nicoll, *A Diary of Public Transactions*, p. 27.

8. Leslie to Argyll, September 5 1650: Robert Kerr, *Correspondence of Sir Robert Kerr first Earl of Ancram and his son William third Earl of Lothian 1616 ...* [1667], ed. D. Laing, 2 vols (Edinburgh, 1875), vol. 2, p. 297.

9. In their descriptions of the battle both Charles Firth and Samuel Gardiner accepted Fitz-Payne Fisher's engraving as accurate, in contrast with the present author's conclusions and those of John Grainger in *Cromwell Against the Scots*, published in 1997.

10. Although C H Firth in his account of the battle ('Site of Battle of Dunbar') takes the picture at face value, due to its number of inaccuracies when compared with contemporary accounts it cannot be relied upon.

11. Hodgson, *Memoirs*, p. 147.

12. A suitable map to use here is the OS Explorer 351 for Dunbar and North Berwick, scale 1:25,000. Ideally it could be used with the 1853 OS Map of Haddingtonshire, scale 6 inches to the mile.

13. Hodgson, *Memoirs*, p. 147.
14. Ibid., p. 279.
15. Ibid., p. 147.
16. Carlyle, *Cromwell's Letters and Speeches*, vol. 2, Letter CXXVII, p. 215.
17. John Rushworth to Speaker Lenthall, *Old Parliamentary History*, vol. 19, p. 341.
18. Carlyle, *Cromwell's Letters and Speeches*, vol. 2, Letter CXXVII, p. 215.

Chapter 9: Capture and Exploitation

1. After the Battle of Naseby Cromwell's troopers (being ordered not to dismount and plunder) followed the fleeing Royalists for fourteen miles, killing them all the way, and after beating the Engagers at Preston Cromwell had Lambert pursuing the broken cavalry to capture its leaders.
2. Carte, *Original Letters and Papers*, vol. 1, p. 383.
3. *Mercurius Politicus*, 12–19 September 1650.
4. Carlyle, *Cromwell's Letters and Speeches*, vol. 2, Letter CXXVII, p. 216.
5. Ibid., p. 209.
6. Carlyle, *Cromwell's Letters and Speeches*, vol. 2, Letter CXXXIX, p. 221.
7. Ibid., p. 222.
8. Ibid.
9. Hodgson, *Memoirs*, pp. 339–46 (letter of Hesilrige to the Council of State dated 31 October 1650).
10. Ibid., p. 343.
11. Ibid., pp. 344–6.
12. Charles Edward Banks, 'Scotch Prisoners deported to New England by Cromwell 1651–2', *Massachusetts Historical Society*, Proceedings, 61 (October 1927) pp. 14, 16.
13. Thomas Hutchinson, *A Collection of Original Papers relative to the History of the Colony of Massachusetts Bay* (Albany, NY, 1865), vol. 2, p. 264 (John Cotton to Cromwell, 1 July 1651).
14. Douglas, *Cromwell's Scotch Campaigns*, p. 112.
15. Pugh, *Swords, Loaves and Fishes*, p. 186.
16. Basil Peacock, *Prisoner on the Kwai* (Bath, 1973), p. 281.
17. *Mercurius Politicus*, 20 September 1650.
18. Royle, *Civil War*, p. 586.
19. Abbott, *Writings and Speeches of Oliver Cromwell*, vol. 2, pp. 359–60.
20. Carlyle, *Cromwell's Letters and Speeches*, vol. 2, Letter CXXVIII, pp. 220–1.
21. Ibid., Letter CXXXVII, pp. 153–4.
22. Walker, *Historical Discourses*, p. 188.
23. Mark Napier, *Memorials of Montrose and his Times*, 2 vols (Edinburgh, Maitland Club, 1848–50), vol. 1, pp. 172–3.
24. Paterson, *A Land Afflicted*, p. 207.
25. Ibid., p. 206.

Chapter 10: Towards Full Conquest

1. Gardiner, *History of the Commonwealth and Protectorate*, p. 297.
2. *Acts of the Parliaments of Scotland*, vol. 2, pp. 654–5.
3. *Mercurius Politicus*, 18–21 February 1651.
4. Grainger, *Cromwell Against the Scots*, p. 90.
5. *Mercurius Politicus*, 20–26 May 1651.
6. *Mercurius Politicus*, 30 May–6 June 1651.
7. Douglas, *Cromwell's Scotch Campaigns*, p. 262.
8. *Calendar of State Papers Domestic* (1651), p. 584.
9. Carlyle, *Cromwell's Letters and Speeches*, vol. 2, Letter CLXVI, pp. 328–9.
10. Buchan, *Oliver Cromwell*, p. 395.
11. *Mercurius Politicus*, 16–23 October 1651.
12. Carlyle, *Cromwell's Letters and Speeches*, vol. 2, p. 334.
13. Ibid., Letter CLXVI, pp. 329, 330.
14. Grainger, *Cromwell Against the Scots*, p. 160.
15. Royle, *Civil War*, p. 606.

Select Bibliography

Acta Parliamentorum Caroli I.

Abbott, W C, *Writings and Speeches of Oliver Cromwell*, 4 vols (Cambridge, MA, 1937–47).

Ashley, Maurice, *The Greatness of Oliver Cromwell* (London, 1959).

——, *Cromwell's Generals* (London, 1954).

Aubrey, John, *Miscellanies upon Various Subjects*, 5th edn (London, 1890).

Baillie, Robert, *The Letters and Journals of Robert Baillie*, ed. D. Laing, 3 vols (Edinburgh, Bannatyne Club, 1841–2).

Baldock, T S, *Cromwell as a Soldier* (1899).

The Basilikon Doron of James VI, ed. James Craigie (Scottish Texts Society, 1944).

Blair, Claude (ed.), *Pollard's History of Firearms* (London, 1983).

Buchan, John, *Montrose* (London, 1927).

——, *Oliver Cromwell* (London, 1934).

Burnet, Bishop Gilbert, *History of His Own Times*, 2 vols (London, 1724–34).

Calendar of State Papers, Domestic, of the reign of Charles I (London, 1858–97).

Calendar of State Papers, Domestic, of the reign of Charles II (London, 1860–1939).

Campbell, A H, *Cromwell's Edinburgh Campaign* (pamphlet, 1854).

Capp, Bernard, *Cromwell's Navy: the Fleet and the English Revolution, 1648–1660* (Oxford, 1989).

Carlson, Stephen P, *The Scots at Hammersmith* (Saugus, MA, 1970).

Carlyle, Thomas, *Oliver Cromwell's Letters and Speeches*, 3 vols (London, 1846).

Carte, Thomas, *A Collection of Original Letters and Papers concerning the Affairs of England from the Year 1641 to 1660*, 2 vols (London, 1739).

Dawson, W H, *Cromwell's Understudy: The Life and Times of General John Lambert* (London, 1938).

Douglas, Sir Robert, *The Peerage of Scotland*, 2 vols (Edinburgh, 1813).

Douglas, W S, *Cromwell's Scotch Campaigns 1650–51* (London, 1898).

Dow, Frances, *Cromwellian Scotland 1651–1660* (Edinburgh, 1999).

Evelyn, John, *The Diary of John Evelyn*, ed. E. S. de Beer, 6 vols (Oxford, 1955).

Exchequer Rolls of Scotland, ed. George Powell McNeill, vol. 18: 1543–1556 (Edinburgh, 1898).

Ferguson, James (ed.), *Papers Illustrating the History of the Scots Brigade in the Service of the United Netherlands 1572–1782*, vol. 1 (Edinburgh, 1899).

Firth, C H, *Oliver Cromwell and the Rule of the Puritans in England* (London, 1923).

——, *Cromwell's Army: A History of the English Soldier during the Civil Wars, the Commonwealth and the Protectorate* (London, 1962).

Fraser, Antonia, *Cromwell, Our Chief of Men* (London, 1973).

Furgol, Edward M, *A Regimental History of the Covenanting Armies 1639–1651* (Edinburgh, 1990).

Gardiner, Samuel R, *History of the Great Civil War 1642–1649*, 4 vols (London, 1886–91).

——, *History of the Commonwealth and Protectorate 1649–1656*, 4 vols (London, 1903).

Gillingham, John, *Cromwell: Portrait of a Soldier* (London, 1976).

Grainger, John D, *Cromwell Against the Scots: The Last Anglo-Scottish War, 1650–1652* (East Linton, 1997).

Gumble, Thomas, *The Life of General Monck, Duke of Albemarle* (London, 1671).

Hall, A R, *Ballistics in the Seventeenth Century* (Cambridge, 1952).

Henry, Chris, *English Civil War Artillery 1642–51* (Oxford, 2005).

Hill, Christopher, *God's Englishman: Oliver Cromwell and the English Revolution* (London, 1970).

Hill, James Michael, *Celtic Warfare 1595–1763* (Edinburgh, 2003).

Hobman, D L, *Cromwell's Master Spy: A Study of John Thurloe* (London, 1961).

Hodgson, John, *Memoirs of Captain John Hodgson* (Edinburgh, 1806).

Hume Brown, P, *The Register of the Privy Council of Scotland*, 2nd Series, vol. 7, 1638–43 (Edinburgh, 1906).

Hyde, Edward, Earl of Clarendon, *The History of the Rebellion and Civil War in England*, ed. W D Macray, 6 vols (Oxford, 1992).

Kitson, Frank, *Old Ironsides: The Military Biography of Oliver Cromwell* (London, 2004).

Leslie, Colonel K H of Balquhain, *Historical Records of the Family of Leslie from 1067–1869*, 2 vols (Edinburgh, 1869).

Lythe, S G E, *The Economy of Scotland in its European Setting* (London, 1960).

McCoy, F N, *Robert Baillie and the Second Scots Reformation* (Berkeley and Los Angeles, 1974).

Macinnes, Allan I, *Charles I and the Making of the Covenanting Movement 1625–1641* (Edinburgh, 2003).

Marshall, Alan, *Oliver Cromwell, Soldier* (London, 2004).

Mercurius Politicus.

Miller, James, *The Lamp of Lothian, or the History of Haddington* (Edinburgh, 1844).

Nicoll, J, *A Diary of Public Transactions and other Occurrences, chiefly in Scotland, from January 1650 to June 1667* (Edinburgh, Bannatyne Club, 1836).

Paterson, Raymond Campbell, *A Land Afflicted: Scotland and the Covenanter Wars 1638–1690* (Edinburgh, 1998).

Paul, Robert S, *The Lord Protector: Religion and Politics in the Life of Oliver Cromwell* (London, 1955).

Peacock, Basil, *Prisoner on the Kwai* (Bath, 1973).

Pepys, Samuel, *The Diary of Samuel Pepys*, ed. Robert Latham and William Matthews (London, 1983).

Phillips, C E Lucas, *Cromwell's Captains* (London and Toronto, 1938).

Pugh, R J M, *Swords, Loaves and Fishes: A History of Dunbar from Earliest Times to the Present* (Balerno, 2003).

Reese, Peter, *The Scottish Commander: Scotland's Greatest Military Leaders from Wallace to World War II* (Edinburgh, 1999).

——, *Flodden: A Scottish Tragedy* (Edinburgh, 2003).

Register of the Privy Council of Scotland, vol. 7, 1638–43 (Edinburgh, 1906).

Reid, Stuart, *Dunbar 1650* (Oxford, 2004).

Reilly, Tom, *Cromwell: An Honourable Enemy. The Untold Story of the Cromwellian Invasion of Ireland* (Dingle, Co. Kerry, 1999).

Robertson, David and Marguerite Wood, *Castle and Town: Chapters in the History of the Royal Burgh of Edinburgh* (London and Edinburgh, 1928).

Royle, Trevor, *Civil War: The Wars of the Three Kingdoms, 1638–1660* (London, 2004).

Rushworth, John, *Historical Collections of Private Passages of State* (London, 1659–1701).

The Scots Peerage, ed. James Balfour Paul, vol. 6 (1909).

Scott, David, *Politics and War in the Three Stuart Kingdoms* (London, 2004).

Simms, J G, *War and Politics in Ireland* (London, 1986).

Skinner, Thomas, *Life of General Monck, Duke of Albemarle* (London, 1724).

Smith, Charles J, *Historic South Edinburgh* (Edinburgh, 2000).

Somers Collection of Tracts. A Collection of Scarce and Valuable Tracts particularly by the late Lord Somers, revised, augmented and arranged by Walter Scott, 8 vols (London, 1812).

Stevenson, David, *Revolution and Counter Revolution in Scotland 1644–1651* (London, 1977).

Stodart, Robert Riddle, *Memorials of the Browns of Fordell, Finmount and Vicarsgrange* (Edinburgh, 1887).

Terry, Charles Sanford, *The Life and Campaigns of Alexander Leslie, First Earl of Leven* (London, 1899).

——, *Papers relating to the Army of the Solemn League and Covenant 1643–47* (Edinburgh, 1917).

Thurloe, John, *A Collection of State Papers of John Thurloe*, 7 vols (London, 1742).

Tincey, John, *Marston Moor 1644: The Beginning of the End* (Oxford, 2003).

Turner, Sir James, *Memoirs of His Own Life and Times 1632–70* (Edinburgh, Bannatyne Club, 1829).

Walker, Sir Edward, *Historical Discourses* (London, 1705).

Wedgwood, C V, *The King's War 1641–1647* (London, 1958).

Wheeler, James Scott, *The Irish and British Wars 1637–1654: Triumph, Tragedy, and Failure* (London, 2002).

Whitelocke, Bulstrode, *Memorials of the English Affairs from the beginning of the Reign of Charles I to King Charles II's Happy Restoration* (London, 1722).

Wilson, A W, *The Story of the Gun* (Woolwich, Royal Artillery Institution, 1944).

Woolrych, Austin, *England without a King 1649–1660* (London, 1993).

Young, Peter, *The English Civil War Armies* (Oxford, 2003).

Young, Peter and Richard Holmes, *The English Civil War* (London, 1974).

Index